Easy And Quick

Air Fryer Cookbook for Beginners UK

Super-Easy, Energy-Saving & Delicious Air Fryer Recipes for Everyday Homemade Meals Incl. Tips and Nutrition Facts | Enhanced with Vibrant Pictures

Valerie T. Barnes

All Rights Reserved.

The contents of this book may not be reproduced, copied or transmitted without the direct written permission of the author or publisher. Under no circumstances will the publisher or the author be held responsible or liable for any damage, compensation or pecuniary loss arising directly or indirectly from the information contained in this book.

Legal notice. This book is protected by copyright. It is intended for personal use only. You may not modify, distribute, sell, use, quote or paraphrase any part or content of this book without the consent of the author or publisher.

Notice Of Disclaimer.

Please note that the information in this document is intended for educational and entertainment purposes only. Every effort has been made to provide accurate, up-to-date, reliable and complete information. No warranty of any kind is declared or implied. The reader acknowledges that the author does not engage in the provision of legal, financial, medical or professional advice. The content in this book has been obtained from a variety of sources. Please consult a licensed professional before attempting any of the techniques described in this book. By reading this document, the reader agrees that in no event shall the author be liable for any direct or indirect damages, including but not limited to errors, omissions or inaccuracies, resulting from the use of the information in this document.

Contents

Introduction 10
- The Rise of Air Fryers: A Brief History and Evolution in British Kitchens 10
- The Science Behind Air Fryer Cooking: A Culinary Revolution 11
- The Versatility of Air Fryers: From Crispy Snacks to Gourmet Meals 12

Bread And Breakfast 13
- Mini Everything Bagels 13
- Nutty Whole Wheat Muffins 13
- Colorful French Toast Sticks 13
- Matcha Granola 14
- Soft Pretzels 14
- Pumpkin Bread With Walnuts 15
- French Toast And Turkey Sausage Roll-ups 15
- Lime Muffins 15
- Easy Caprese Flatbread 16
- Cheddar-ham-corn Muffins 16
- Orange Rolls 17
- Bagels With Avocado & Tomatoes 17
- Mediterranean Egg Sandwich 17
- Chocolate Chip Banana Muffins 18
- Breakfast Chimichangas 18
- Huevos Rancheros 18
- Zucchini Hash Browns 19
- Hashbrown Potatoes Lyonnaise 19
- Crispy Chicken Cakes 20
- Green Egg Quiche 20

Appetizers And Snacks 21
- Hot Garlic Kale Chips 21
- Jalapeño & Mozzarella Stuffed Mushrooms 21
- Sweet-and-salty Pretzels 21
- Turkey Bacon Dates 22

Kale Chips 22
Poppy Seed Mini Hot Dog Rolls 22
Garam Masala Cauliflower Pakoras 23
Crispy Curried Sweet Potato Fries 23
Roasted Red Pepper Dip 23
Fried Olives 24
Fried Peaches 24
Shrimp Pirogues 25
Roasted Tomatillo Salsa 25
Rosemary Garlic Goat Cheese 26
Avocado Fries 26
Zucchini Fries With Roasted Garlic Aïoli 26
Thick-crust Pepperoni Pizza 27
Carrot Chips 27
Buffalo Bites 27
Ranch Chips 28

Poultry Recipes 29

Chicken Souvlaki Gyros 29
Yogurt-marinated Chicken Legs 29
Philly Chicken Cheesesteak Stromboli 29
Jerk Chicken Drumsticks 30
Turkey-hummus Wraps 31
Southern-fried Chicken Livers 31
Japanese-style Turkey Meatballs 31
Fennel & Chicken Ratatouille 32
Asian Sweet Chili Chicken 32
Chicken Meatballs With A Surprise 32
Chicken Parmesan 33
Chicken Cordon Bleu Patties 33
Crispy Duck With Cherry Sauce 34
Tortilla Crusted Chicken Breast 34
Air-fried Turkey Breast With Cherry Glaze 34
Windsor's Chicken Salad 35

Gingery Turkey Meatballs 35
Pecan Turkey Cutlets 36
Katsu Chicken Thighs 36
Curried Chicken Legs 37

Beef, Pork & Lamb Recipes 37

Steakhouse Burgers With Red Onion Compote 37
Wasabi-coated Pork Loin Chops 38
Broccoli & Mushroom Beef 38
Basil Cheese & Ham Stromboli 38
Sloppy Joes 39
Honey Mustard Pork Roast 39
Original Köttbullar 39
Tandoori Lamb Samosas 40
Country-style Pork Ribs(2) 40
Aromatic Pork Tenderloin 41
Beef Fajitas 41
Crispy Smoked Pork Chops 41
French-style Pork Medallions 42
Pork & Beef Egg Rolls 42
Boneless Ribeyes 43
Coffee-rubbed Pork Tenderloin 43
Orange Glazed Pork Tenderloin 43
Apple Cornbread Stuffed Pork Loin With Apple Gravy 44
Easy Tex-mex Chimichangas 45
Extra Crispy Country-style Pork Riblets 45

Fish And Seafood Recipes 46

Sesame-crusted Tuna Steaks 46
Easy Scallops With Lemon Butter 46
Saucy Shrimp 46
French Grouper Nicoise 47
Feta & Shrimp Pita 47
Buttered Swordfish Steaks 47

Kid's Flounder Fingers 48
Shrimp Po'boy With Remoulade Sauce 48
Basil Crab Cakes With Fresh Salad 48
Mahi Mahi With Cilantro-chili Butter 49
Fish-in-chips 49
Potato-wrapped Salmon Fillets 50
Holiday Lobster Salad 50
Fish Tortillas With Coleslaw 50
Fish Cakes 51
Old Bay Fish `n´ Chips 51
Garlic-butter Lobster Tails 52
British Fish & Chips 52
Maple Balsamic Glazed Salmon 52
Californian Tilapia 53

Vegetarian Recipes 54

Easy Zucchini Lasagna Roll-ups 54
Fake Shepherd´s Pie 54
Crunchy Rice Paper Samosas 54
Cheesy Veggie Frittata 55
Eggplant Parmesan 55
Cheddar Bean Taquitos 56
Basil Green Beans 56
Home-style Cinnamon Rolls 56
Hearty Salad 56
Spiced Vegetable Galette 57
Sushi-style Deviled Eggs 57
Tex-mex Potatoes With Avocado Dressing 58
Cheesy Eggplant Rounds 58
Golden Breaded Mushrooms 58
Sweet Corn Bread 59
Vegetarian Stuffed Bell Peppers 59
Stuffed Zucchini Boats 60
Veggie-stuffed Bell Peppers 60

Sesame Orange Tofu With Snow Peas 60
Two-cheese Grilled Sandwiches 61

Vegetable Side Dishes Recipes 62

Southern Okra Chips 62
Crispy Herbed Potatoes 62
Roasted Corn Salad 62
Mediterranean Roasted Vegetables 63
Steak Fries 63
Balsamic Beet Chips 63
Pork Tenderloin Salad 64
Wilted Brussels Sprout Slaw 64
Mom's Potatoes Au Gratin 65
Acorn Squash Halves With Maple Butter Glaze 65
Best-ever Brussels Sprouts 65
Dilly Sesame Roasted Asparagus 66
Herbed Zucchini Poppers 66
Tandoori Cauliflower 66
Steakhouse Baked Potatoes 67
Honey-mustard Roasted Cabbage 67
Mushrooms, Sautéed 67
Onion Rings 68
Rich Baked Sweet Potatoes 68
Five-spice Roasted Sweet Potatoes 68

Sandwiches And Burgers Recipes 69

Thai-style Pork Sliders 69
Dijon Thyme Burgers 69
Reuben Sandwiches 70
Lamb Burgers 70
Asian Glazed Meatballs 71
Chicken Saltimbocca Sandwiches 72
Black Bean Veggie Burgers 72
Perfect Burgers 73

Salmon Burgers 73
Provolone Stuffed Meatballs 74
Inside-out Cheeseburgers 74
Chicken Club Sandwiches 75
Mexican Cheeseburgers 75
Eggplant Parmesan Subs 76
Best-ever Roast Beef Sandwiches 76
Chili Cheese Dogs 77
White Bean Veggie Burgers 77
Crunchy Falafel Balls 78
Sausage And Pepper Heros 78

Desserts And Sweets 79

Holiday Peppermint Cake 79
Mango Cobbler With Raspberries 79
Dark Chocolate Cream Galette 79
Apple Dumplings 80
Donut Holes 80
Coconut-custard Pie 81
Giant Buttery Chocolate Chip Cookie 81
Spanish Churro Bites 82
Struffoli 82
Sea-salted Caramel Cookie Cups 83
Glazed Cherry Turnovers 83
Nutty Cookies 84
Orange-chocolate Cake 84
Mom's Amaretto Cheesecake 84
Fried Twinkies 85
Sultana & Walnut Stuffed Apples 85
Mango-chocolate Custard 86
Fast Brownies 86
Honeyed Tortilla Fritters 86
Vanilla-strawberry Muffins 87

INDEX 88

Measurement and Conversion

Weight Measurements:
1 ounce (oz) = 28 grams (g)
1 pound (lb) = 16 ounces (oz) = 454 grams (g)
1 stone = 14 pounds (lb) = 6.35 kilograms (kg)

Volume Measurements:
1 teaspoon (tsp) = 5 milliliters (ml)
1 tablespoon (tbsp) = 15 milliliters (ml)
1 fluid ounce (fl oz) = 28 milliliters (ml)
1 cup = 8 fluid ounces (fl oz) = 240 milliliters (ml)
1 pint (pt) = 20 fluid ounces (fl oz) = 568 milliliters (ml)
1 quart (qt) = 2 pints (pt) = 40 fluid ounces (fl oz) = 1.137 liters (L)
1 gallon (gal) = 4 quarts (qt) = 8 pints (pt) = 160 fluid ounces (fl oz) = 4.546 liters (L)

Lengths Measurements:
1 inch (in) = 2.54 centimeters (cm)
1 meter (m) = 100 centimeters (cm) = 39.37 inches (in)
1 kilometer (km) = 1,000 meters (m) = 0.62 miles (mi)
1 mile (mi) = 1.61 kilometers (km)

Introduction

The Rise of Air Fryers: A Brief History and Evolution in British Kitchens

Air fryers have taken the British culinary scene by storm in recent years, offering a healthier and more convenient alternative to traditional deep frying. These innovative appliances have quickly become a staple in many households, revolutionising the way we prepare our favourite fried dishes.

Air fryers first emerged in the early 2010s, with Philips introducing the first commercially available model in 2010. The concept behind air fryers was to simulate the crispy texture and golden-brown appearance of deep-fried foods using hot air circulation and minimal oil. This new cooking method appealed to health-conscious consumers seeking to reduce their intake of fat and calories without compromising on taste.

As awareness of the benefits of air frying spread, British consumers began to embrace this new cooking appliance. The demand for air fryers in the UK market grew steadily, with sales increasing year on year. By the mid-2010s, air fryers had become a common sight in British kitchens, with various brands and models available to suit different budgets and cooking needs.

Over the years, air fryer technology has continued to evolve and improve. Manufacturers have introduced new features and functionalities to enhance the cooking experience and versatility of these appliances. Some notable advancements include digital displays and touch controls for precise temperature and timing settings, larger capacity baskets to accommodate family-sized portions, multiple cooking functions such as roasting, grilling, and baking, pre-programmed cooking modes for specific food items, and improved air circulation systems for even cooking results.

The popularity of air fryers has significantly influenced the British recipe market. Food bloggers, chefs, and home cooks have embraced this new cooking method, developing a wide range of air fryer recipes tailored to British tastes and preferences. From classic fish and chips to Yorkshire puddings and roasted vegetables, air fryers have allowed for healthier versions of traditional British dishes.

Additionally, the convenience and versatility of air fryers have inspired the creation of new and innovative recipes. Home cooks have experimented with air frying everything from stuffed mushrooms and scotch eggs to fruit crumbles and cakes. The air fryer has become a tool for culinary creativity, enabling the development of unique and exciting dishes.

The rise of air fryers in the British recipe market has been a testament to the growing demand for healthier and more convenient cooking options. From their inception in the early 2010s to their current status as a kitchen essential, air fryers have transformed the way Britons prepare and enjoy their favourite fried foods. As technology continues to advance and new recipes emerge, it is clear that air fryers will remain a significant influence on British culinary culture for years to come.

The Science Behind Air Fryer Cooking: A Culinary Revolution

Air fryers have taken the culinary world by storm, offering a healthier and more efficient way to enjoy our favorite fried foods. But what exactly is the science behind this innovative appliance? Let's explore the fascinating technology that powers the air fryer and discover how it achieves those crispy, golden-brown results.

At the core of an air fryer's operation is a combination of rapid hot air circulation and radiant heat. The appliance is equipped with a powerful heating element, typically located at the top of the unit, which generates intense heat. A built-in fan then circulates this hot air around the cooking chamber at high speeds, creating a miniature convection oven.

As the heated air swirls around the food, it forms a thin, even layer of heat that envelops the entire surface. This process, known as the Maillard reaction, is responsible for the browning and crisping of the food's exterior. The Maillard reaction occurs when amino acids and sugars in the food are exposed to high temperatures, causing them to interact and create complex flavors and aromas.

Simultaneously, the rapid air circulation also facilitates the evaporation of moisture from the food's surface. As the moisture evaporates, it creates a crispy, crunchy texture reminiscent of deep-fried foods. This process is enhanced by the perforated design of the air fryer basket, which allows hot air to penetrate the food from all angles, ensuring even cooking and crispiness.

One of the most significant advantages of air fryer cooking is the reduced need for oil. Unlike traditional deep-frying, which requires food to be submerged in hot oil, air fryers typically require only a small amount of oil, if any at all. The hot air circulation is powerful enough to create a crispy exterior without the need for excessive oil, resulting in a healthier cooking method that reduces fat and calorie intake.

The temperature control in air fryers is another crucial aspect of their operation. Most models allow users to adjust the cooking temperature, typically ranging from 175° C to 200° C (350° F to 400° F). This precise temperature control enables users to customize the cooking process based on the type of food and desired level of crispiness. By adjusting the temperature and cooking time, users can achieve optimal results for a wide variety of dishes, from tender meats to crispy vegetables.

In addition to the convection heating and temperature control, air fryers also benefit from their compact and enclosed design. The small cooking chamber concentrates the heat, allowing for faster cooking times compared to traditional ovens. This efficiency not only saves time but also helps to retain the food's natural flavors and juices, resulting in more flavorful and moist dishes.

The science behind air fryer cooking is a testament to human ingenuity and the constant pursuit of culinary innovation. By harnessing the power of rapid hot air circulation, radiant heat, and precise temperature control, air fryers have revolutionized the way we prepare our favorite fried foods. With the ability to create crispy, golden-brown exteriors while minimizing oil usage, air fryers offer a healthier and more efficient cooking method that doesn't compromise on taste or texture.

As more people discover the incredible benefits of air fryer cooking, this appliance is sure to become a staple in kitchens around the world. Whether you're a health-conscious individual looking to reduce your fat intake or a busy home cook seeking a faster and more convenient way to prepare meals, the air fryer is an invaluable tool that combines science and culinary artistry to deliver truly exceptional results.

The Versatility of Air Fryers: From Crispy Snacks to Gourmet Meals

Air fryers have gained immense popularity in recent years, and for good reason. These innovative appliances are not only known for their ability to create healthier versions of our favorite fried foods but also for their incredible versatility in the kitchen. From crispy snacks to gourmet meals, the air fryer has become a go-to tool for home cooks looking to expand their culinary repertoire.

One of the most obvious and well-known uses for air fryers is creating crispy, golden-brown snacks and appetizers. Whether you're craving classic french fries, zucchini sticks, or mozzarella bites, the air fryer can deliver that satisfying crunch without the need for deep-frying. By using just a small amount of oil and the power of rapid hot air circulation, the air fryer achieves a crispy exterior while keeping the interior moist and tender.

But the versatility of air fryers extends far beyond just snacks and appetizers. These appliances are also capable of cooking a wide variety of main dishes, from juicy proteins to tender vegetables. Imagine perfectly cooked chicken breasts with a crispy, golden-brown skin or succulent pork chops that are tender on the inside and crispy on the outside. The air fryer's ability to quickly and evenly cook proteins makes it an ideal choice for busy weeknight dinners.

Vegetarians and vegans can also benefit from the air fryer's versatility. The appliance is perfect for roasting vegetables, creating crispy tofu, or even preparing plant-based burgers and nuggets. The hot air circulation ensures that vegetables are cooked evenly, retaining their natural flavors and nutrients while developing a delightful crispy texture.

For those with a sweet tooth, the air fryer can even be used to create delectable desserts. From air-fried donuts and churros to fruit crisps and mini pies, the possibilities are endless. The air fryer's ability to create a crispy exterior while keeping the interior soft and gooey makes it perfect for satisfying your sweet cravings without the guilt associated with deep-fried treats.

The air fryer's versatility also extends to its ability to reheat leftovers. Say goodbye to soggy, microwaved food and hello to crispy, revitalized leftovers. Whether it's pizza, fried chicken, or even French fries, the air fryer can bring your leftover dishes back to life, restoring their original crunch and flavor.

One of the most significant advantages of the air fryer's versatility is its ability to simplify meal preparation. With just one appliance, you can cook a complete meal, from appetizers to main courses and even desserts. This not only saves time but also reduces the number of dishes and utensils needed, making cleanup a breeze.

As home cooks continue to explore the vast potential of air fryers, the culinary possibilities are endless. From experimenting with new recipes to putting unique twists on classic dishes, the air fryer encourages creativity and innovation in the kitchen. With its ability to cook a wide range of foods in a healthier and more efficient manner, the air fryer has become an indispensable tool for those looking to elevate their cooking game.

The versatility of air fryers is a testament to their incredible capabilities and the ingenuity of modern cooking technology. Whether you're a busy parent looking for quick and healthy meal options, a fitness enthusiast seeking to maintain a balanced diet, or a foodie eager to explore new culinary horizons, the air fryer is an appliance that can cater to your every need. Embrace the versatility of this incredible appliance and discover a world of crispy, delicious, and healthier cooking possibilities.

Bread And Breakfast

Mini Everything Bagels

Servings: 4 | Prep Time: 15 Minutes | Cooking Time: 6 Minutes

Ingredients:

- 1 cup all-purpose flour
- 2 teaspoons baking powder
- ½ teaspoon salt
- 1 cup plain Greek yogurt
- 1 egg, whisked
- 1 teaspoon sesame seeds
- 1 teaspoon dehydrated onions
- ½ teaspoon poppy seeds
- ½ teaspoon garlic powder
- ½ teaspoon sea salt flakes

Directions:

1. In a large bowl, mix together the flour, baking powder, and salt. Make a well in the dough and add in the Greek yogurt. Mix with a spoon until a dough forms.
2. Place the dough onto a heavily floured surface and knead for 3 minutes. You may use up to 1 cup of additional flour as you knead the dough, if necessary.
3. Cut the dough into 8 pieces and roll each piece into a 15-cm, snakelike piece. Touch the ends of each piece together so it closes the circle and forms a bagel shape. Brush the tops of the bagels with the whisked egg.
4. In a small bowl, combine the sesame seeds, dehydrated onions, poppy seeds, garlic powder, and sea salt flakes. Sprinkle the seasoning on top of the bagels.
5. Preheat the air fryer to 180°C/360°F. Using a bench scraper or flat-edged spatula, carefully place the bagels into the air fryer basket. Spray the bagel tops with cooking spray. Air-fry the bagels for 6 minutes or until golden brown. Allow the bread to cool at least 10 minutes before slicing for serving.

Variations & Ingredients Tips:

- Use whole wheat flour for a more nutritious bagel.
- Add dried herbs like rosemary or thyme to the seasoning mix.
- Top with cream cheese or your favorite bagel spread.

Per serving: Calories: 264; Total Fat: 3.5g; Saturated Fat: 1.1g; Cholesterol: 51mg; Sodium: 609mg; Total Carbohydrates: 44.9g; Dietary Fiber: 1.6g; Total Sugars: 2.8g; Protein: 11.7g

Nutty Whole Wheat Muffins

Servings: 8 | Prep Time: 15 Minutes | Cooking Time: 11 Minutes

Ingredients:

- ½ cup + 2 tbsp whole-wheat flour
- ¼ cup oat bran
- 2 tbsp flaxseed meal
- ¼ cup brown sugar
- ½ tsp baking soda
- ½ tsp baking powder
- ¼ tsp salt
- ½ tsp cinnamon
- ½ cup buttermilk
- 2 tbsp melted butter
- 1 egg
- ½ tsp pure vanilla extract
- ½ cup grated carrots
- ¼ cup chopped pecans
- ¼ cup chopped walnuts
- 1 tbsp pumpkin seeds
- 1 tbsp sunflower seeds
- 16 foil muffin cups, paper liners removed
- Cooking spray

Directions:

1. Preheat air fryer to 165°C/330°F.
2. In a large bowl, stir together the flour, bran, flaxseed meal, sugar, baking soda, baking powder, salt, and cinnamon.
3. In a medium bowl, beat together the buttermilk, butter, egg, and vanilla. Pour into flour mixture and stir just until dry ingredients moisten. Do not beat.
4. Gently stir in carrots, nuts, and seeds.
5. Double up the foil cups so you have 8 total and spray with cooking spray.
6. Place 4 foil cups in air fryer basket and divide half the batter among them.
7. Cook at 165°C/330°F for 11 minutes or until toothpick inserted in center comes out clean.
8. Repeat step 7 to cook remaining 4 muffins.

Variations & Ingredients Tips:

- Use different nuts like almonds or hazelnuts.
- Replace carrots with grated zucchini or apple.
- Drizzle with a cream cheese glaze after baking.

Per serving: Calories: 198; Total Fat: 10.9g; Saturated Fat: 2.6g; Cholesterol: 30mg; Sodium: 199mg; Total Carbohydrates: 22.8g; Dietary Fiber: 3.9g; Total Sugars: 9.2g; Protein: 4.8g

Colorful French Toast Sticks

Servings: 4 | Prep Time: 10 Minutes | Cooking Time: 20 Minutes

Ingredients:

- 1 egg
- ⅓ cup whole milk
- Salt to taste
- ½ teaspoon ground cinnamon
- ½ teaspoon ground chia seeds
- 1 cup crushed pebbles
- 4 sandwich bread slices, each cut into 4 sticks
- ¼ cup honey

Directions:

1. Preheat air fryer at 190°C/375°F.
2. Whisk the egg, milk, salt, cinnamon and chia seeds in a bowl. In another bowl, add crushed cereal.
3. Dip breadsticks in the egg mixture, then dredge them in the cereal crumbs.
4. Place breadsticks in the greased frying basket and Air Fry for 5 minutes, flipping once.
5. Serve with honey as a dip.

Variations & Ingredients Tips:

- ▶ Use different types of bread, such as whole wheat or brioche, for a variety of flavors and textures.
- ▶ Add some vanilla extract or orange zest to the egg mixture for extra flavor.
- ▶ For a savory version, replace the cinnamon and honey with garlic powder and marinara sauce for dipping.

Per Serving: Calories: 240; Total Fat: 5g; Saturated Fat: 1.5g; Cholesterol: 50mg; Sodium: 330mg; Total Carbs: 43g; Fiber: 2g; Sugars: 18g; Protein: 7g

Matcha Granola

Servings: 4 | Prep Time: 10 Minutes | Cooking Time: 15 Minutes

Ingredients:

- 2 tsp matcha green tea
- 1/2 cup slivered almonds
- 1/2 cup pecan pieces
- 1/2 cup sunflower seeds
- 1/2 cup pumpkin seeds
- 1 cup coconut flakes
- 1/4 cup coconut sugar
- 1/8 cup flour
- 1/8 cup almond flour
- 1 tsp vanilla extract
- 2 tbsp melted butter
- 2 tbsp almond butter
- 1/8 tsp salt

Directions:

1. Preheat air fryer to 150°C/300°F.
2. Mix the green tea, almonds, pecan, sunflower seeds, pumpkin seeds, coconut flakes, sugar, flour, almond flour, vanilla extract, butter, almond butter, and salt in a bowl.
3. Spoon the mixture into an ungreased round 4-cup baking dish. Place it in the fryer and Bake for 6 minutes, stirring once.
4. Transfer to an airtight container, let cool for 10 minutes, then cover and store at room temperature until ready to serve.

Variations & Ingredients Tips:

- ▶ Use cashews, macadamia nuts or Brazil nuts instead of pecans.
- ▶ Add some dried fruit like goji berries, mulberries or goldenberries.
- ▶ Serve with milk, yogurt or as a topping for smoothie bowls.

Per serving: Calories: 630; Total Fat: 52g; Saturated Fat: 19g; Cholesterol: 30mg; Sodium: 160mg; Total Carbs: 35g; Dietary Fiber: 9g; Total Sugars: 16g; Protein: 13g

Soft Pretzels

Servings: 12 | Prep Time: 20 Minutes | Cooking Time: 6 Minutes

Ingredients:

- 2 teaspoons yeast
- 1 cup water, warm
- 1 teaspoon sugar
- 1 teaspoon salt
- 2½ cups all-purpose flour
- 2 tablespoons butter, melted
- 1 cup boiling water
- 1 tablespoon baking soda
- coarse sea salt
- melted butter

Directions:

1. Combine yeast and warm water in a small bowl.
2. In mixer bowl, mix sugar, salt and flour. With mixer running, add yeast mix and melted butter. Knead 10 mins.
3. Shape into a ball, let rise 1 hour.
4. Punch down dough and divide into 12-48 pieces depending on desired pretzel size.
5. Roll each into a rope and shape into pretzel/knot.
6. Combine boiling water and baking soda in a bowl. Let cool slightly.
7. Working in batches, dip pretzels in baking soda water for 30-60 secs then place on parchment. Sprinkle with salt.
8. Preheat air fryer to 175°C/350°F. Air fry in batches for 3 mins per side.
9. Brush pretzels with melted butter when done.

Variations & Ingredients Tips:

- ▶ Add cheese, herbs or spices to the dough before shaping.

▶ Substitute some of the all-purpose flour with whole wheat.

▶ Serve with mustard, cheese sauce or other dipping sauces.

Per Serving: Calories: 118; Total Fat: 2g; Saturated Fat: 1g; Cholesterol: 5mg; Sodium: 706mg; Total Carbs: 21g; Dietary Fiber: 1g; Total Sugars: 0g; Protein: 3g

Pumpkin Bread With Walnuts

Servings: 6 | Prep Time: 10 Minutes | Cooking Time: 30 Minutes

Ingredients:

- 1/2 cup canned pumpkin puree
- 1 cup flour
- 1/2 tsp baking soda
- 1/2 cup granulated sugar
- 1 tsp pumpkin pie spice
- 1/4 tsp nutmeg
- 1/4 tsp salt
- 1 egg
- 1 tbsp vegetable oil
- 1 tbsp orange juice
- 1 tsp orange zest
- 1/4 cup crushed walnuts

Directions:

1. Preheat air fryer at 190°C/375°F.
2. In a bowl, mix flour, baking soda, sugar, spices, salt, pumpkin, egg, oil, orange juice, zest and walnuts.
3. Pour into a greased cake pan.
4. Place pan in air fryer basket and bake for 20 minutes.
5. Let cool 10 minutes before slicing and serving.

Variations & Ingredients Tips:

▶ Use pecans or a mix of nuts instead of walnuts.

▶ Drizzle with a powdered sugar glaze after baking.

▶ Add chocolate chips or raisins to the batter.

Per serving: Calories: 200; Total Fat: 6g; Saturated Fat: 1g; Cholesterol: 25mg; Sodium: 195mg; Total Carbs: 35g; Dietary Fiber: 2g; Sugars: 18g; Protein: 3g

French Toast And Turkey Sausage Roll-ups

Servings: 3 | Prep Time: 10 Minutes | Cooking Time: 24 Minutes

Ingredients:

- 6 links turkey sausage
- 6 slices of white bread, crusts removed*
- 2 eggs
- 118 ml milk
- 1/2 teaspoon ground cinnamon
- 1/2 teaspoon vanilla extract
- 1 tablespoon butter, melted
- powdered sugar (optional)
- maple syrup

Directions:

1. Preheat the air fryer to 190°C/380°F and pour a little water into the bottom of the air fryer drawer. (This will help prevent the grease that drips into the bottom drawer from burning and smoking.)
2. Air-fry the sausage links at 190°C/380°F for 8 to 10 minutes, turning them a couple of times during the cooking process. (If you have pre-cooked sausage links, omit this step.)
3. Roll each sausage link in a piece of bread, pressing the finished seam tightly to seal shut.
4. Preheat the air fryer to 190°C/370°F.
5. Combine the eggs, milk, cinnamon, and vanilla in a shallow dish. Dip the sausage rolls in the egg mixture and let them soak in the egg for 30 seconds. Spray or brush the bottom of the air fryer basket with oil and transfer the sausage rolls to the basket, seam side down.
6. Air-fry the rolls at 190°C/370°F for 9 minutes. Brush melted butter over the bread, flip the rolls over and air-fry for an additional 5 minutes. Remove the French toast roll-ups from the basket and dust with powdered sugar, if using. Serve with maple syrup and enjoy.

Variations & Ingredients Tips:

▶ Use pork or veggie sausage instead of turkey for different flavors.

▶ Stuff the rolls with a slice of cheese before air frying for a gooey filling.

▶ Sprinkle with chopped nuts, coconut flakes or mini chocolate chips for extra texture.

Per Serving: Calories: 416; Total Fat: 24g; Saturated Fat: 8g; Cholesterol: 185mg; Sodium: 799mg; Total Carbs: 31g; Dietary Fiber: 1g; Total Sugars: 7g; Protein: 19g

Lime Muffins

Servings: 6 | Prep Time: 15 Minutes | Cooking Time: 30 Minutes

Ingredients:

- 1 1/2 tbsp butter, softened
- 6 tbsp sugar
- 1 egg
- 1 egg white

- 1 tsp vanilla extract
- 1 tsp lime juice
- 1 lime, zested
- 150g Greek yogurt
- ¾ cup + 2 tbsp flour
- ¾ cup raspberries

Directions:

1. Beat butter and sugar in a mixer for 2 minutes at medium speed. In a separate bowl, whisk together the egg, egg white and vanilla. Pour into the mixer bowl, add lime juice and zest. Beat until combined. At a low speed, add yogurt then flour.
2. Fold in the raspberries. Divide the mixture into 6 greased muffin cups using an ice cream scoop. The cups should be filled about ¾ of the way.
3. Preheat air fryer to 150°C/300°F. Put the muffins into the air fryer and Bake for 15 minutes until the tops are golden and a toothpick in the center comes out clean.
4. Allow to cool before serving.

Variations & Ingredients Tips:

- ▶ Use lemon instead of lime for a different citrus flavor.
- ▶ Add some poppy seeds or shredded coconut to the batter.
- ▶ Top with a lime glaze made of powdered sugar and lime juice.

Per serving: Calories: 200; Total Fat: 6g; Saturated Fat: 3g; Cholesterol: 40mg; Sodium: 55mg; Total Carbs: 32g; Dietary Fiber: 2g; Total Sugars: 19g; Protein: 6g

Easy Caprese Flatbread

Servings: 2 | Prep Time: 5 Minutes | Cooking Time: 15 Minutes

Ingredients:

- 1 fresh mozzarella ball, sliced
- 1 flatbread
- 2 teaspoons olive oil
- ¼ garlic clove, minced
- 1 egg
- ⅛ teaspoon salt
- 60 g diced tomato
- 6 basil leaves
- ½ teaspoon dried oregano
- ½ teaspoon balsamic vinegar

Directions:

1. Preheat air fryer to 190°C/380°F.
2. Lightly brush the top of the bread with olive oil, then top with garlic.
3. Crack the egg into a small bowl and sprinkle with salt. Place the bread into the frying basket and gently pour the egg onto the top of the pita. Top with tomato, mozzarella, oregano and basil.
4. Bake for 6 minutes. When ready, remove the pita pizza and drizzle with balsamic vinegar.
5. Let it cool for 5 minutes. Slice and serve.

Variations & Ingredients Tips:

- ▶ Use different types of cheese, such as feta or goat cheese, for a variety of flavors.
- ▶ Add some sliced prosciutto or salami for a meaty twist.
- ▶ For a vegan version, replace the egg and cheese with hummus and sliced avocado.

Per Serving: Calories: 290; Total Fat: 16g; Saturated Fat: 7g; Cholesterol: 105mg; Sodium: 480mg; Total Carbs: 23g; Fiber: 1g; Sugars: 2g; Protein: 14g

Cheddar-ham-corn Muffins

Servings: 8 | Prep Time: 10 Minutes | Cooking Time: 8 Minutes

Ingredients:

- ¾ cup yellow cornmeal
- ¼ cup all-purpose flour
- 1½ teaspoons baking powder
- ¼ teaspoon salt
- 1 egg, beaten
- 2 tablespoons canola oil
- ½ cup milk
- ½ cup shredded sharp Cheddar cheese
- ½ cup diced ham
- 8 foil muffin cups, liners removed and sprayed with cooking spray

Directions:

1. Preheat air fryer to 198°C/390°F.
2. In a bowl, stir together cornmeal, flour, baking powder and salt.
3. Add egg, oil and milk to dry ingredients and mix well.
4. Stir in cheese and diced ham.
5. Divide batter among muffin cups.
6. Place 4 cups in air fryer basket and bake 5 minutes.
7. Reduce temp to 165°C/330°F and bake 1-2 more minutes until a toothpick comes out clean.
8. Repeat with remaining 4 muffins.

Variations & Ingredients Tips:

- ▶ Use bacon or sausage instead of ham.
- ▶ Substitute jalapeños for bell peppers for a spicy version.
- ▶ Add diced onions or scallions to the batter.

Per Serving: Calories: 180; Total Fat: 8g; Saturated Fat: 2g; Cholesterol: 40mg; Sodium:

340mg; Total Carbs: 19g; Dietary Fiber: 1g; Total Sugars: 2g; Protein: 7g

Orange Rolls

Servings: 8 | Prep Time: 15 Minutes | Cooking Time: 10 Minutes

Ingredients:

- Parchment paper
- 85-g low-fat cream cheese
- 1 tbsp low-fat sour cream or plain yogurt
- 2 tsp sugar
- 1/4 tsp vanilla extract
- 1/4 tsp orange extract
- 1 (8 count) can organic crescent roll dough
- 1/4 cup chopped walnuts
- 1/4 cup dried cranberries
- 1/4 cup shredded sweetened coconut
- Butter-flavored cooking spray
- Orange Glaze:
- 1/2 cup powdered sugar
- 1 tbsp orange juice
- 1/4 tsp orange extract
- Dash of salt

Directions:

1. Cut parchment for air fryer basket and set aside.
2. Mix cream cheese, sour cream/yogurt, sugar, vanilla and orange extracts until smooth.
3. Preheat air fryer to 150°C/300°F.
4. Separate crescent dough into triangles. Spread cheese mix on each leaving 2.5cm border.
5. Sprinkle nuts, cranberries over cheese. Roll up from wide end.
6. Place on parchment, spray tops with cooking spray.
7. Air fry 4 rolls for 10 mins until golden.
8. Repeat with remaining rolls.
9. Make glaze and drizzle over warm rolls.

Variations & Ingredients Tips:

▶ Use different dried fruits or nuts.
▶ Substitute almond or lemon extract.
▶ Dust with powdered sugar instead of glaze.

Per Serving: Calories: 220; Total Fat: 12g; Saturated Fat: 4g; Cholesterol: 10mg; Sodium: 230mg; Total Carbs: 26g; Dietary Fiber: 1g; Sugars: 13g; Protein: 3g

Bagels With Avocado & Tomatoes

Servings: 2 | Prep Time: 20 Minutes | Cooking Time: 35 Minutes

Ingredients:

- 2/3 cup all-purpose flour
- 1/2 tsp active dry yeast
- 1/3 cup Greek yogurt
- 8 cherry tomatoes
- 1 ripe avocado
- 1 tbsp lemon juice
- 2 tbsp chopped red onions
- Black pepper to taste

Directions:

1. Preheat air fryer to 205°C/400°F. Beat flour, yeast, and yogurt into a dough, adding more flour if needed. Make 2 balls.
2. Roll each into a 23cm strip and form rings, pressing ends together to make 2 bagels. Soak in hot water 1 min.
3. Drain and let bagels rise 15 mins in fryer. Bake 5 mins, flip, top with tomatoes and bake 5 more mins.
4. Make guacamole: Mash avocado flesh with lemon juice and onions.
5. Cut bagels in half and spread with guacamole. Top with baked tomatoes and black pepper.

Variations & Ingredients Tips:

▶ Use whole wheat or alternative flour for the bagels.
▶ Mix chopped jalapeño or cilantro into the guacamole.
▶ Top with sliced hard boiled eggs for extra protein.

Per Serving: Calories: 410; Total Fat: 12g; Saturated Fat: 2g; Cholesterol: 0mg; Sodium: 135mg; Total Carbs: 65g; Dietary Fiber: 9g; Total Sugars: 5g; Protein: 13g

Mediterranean Egg Sandwich

Servings: 1 | Prep Time: 5 Minutes | Cooking Time: 8 Minutes

Ingredients:

- 1 large egg
- 5 baby spinach leaves, chopped
- 1 tablespoon roasted bell pepper, chopped
- 1 English muffin
- 1 thin slice prosciutto or Canadian bacon

Directions:

1. Spray a ramekin with cooking spray or brush the inside with extra-virgin olive oil.
2. In a small bowl, whisk together the egg, baby spinach, and bell pepper.
3. Split the English muffin in half and spray the inside lightly with cooking spray or brush with extra-virgin olive oil.
4. Preheat the air fryer to 175°C/350°F for 2 minutes. Place the egg ramekin and open English muffin into the air fryer basket, and cook at 175°C/350°F for 5 minutes. Open the air fryer drawer and add the prosciutto or ba-

17

con; cook for an additional 1 minute.

5. To assemble the sandwich, place the egg on one half of the English muffin, top with prosciutto or bacon, and place the remaining piece of English muffin on top.

Variations & Ingredients Tips:

- Add some sliced avocado or tomato to the sandwich.
- Use a bagel or croissant instead of an English muffin.
- Sprinkle with hot sauce or everything bagel seasoning.

Per serving: Calories: 310; Total Fat: 14g; Saturated Fat: 4.5g; Cholesterol: 235mg; Sodium: 830mg; Total Carbs: 27g; Dietary Fiber: 2g; Total Sugars: 3g; Protein: 19g

Chocolate Chip Banana Muffins

Servings: 12 | Prep Time: 10 Minutes | Cooking Time: 14 Minutes

Ingredients:

- 2 medium bananas, mashed
- ¼ cup brown sugar
- 1½ teaspoons vanilla extract
- ⅔ cup milk
- 2 tablespoons butter
- 1 large egg
- 1 cup white whole-wheat flour
- ½ cup old-fashioned oats
- 1 teaspoon baking soda
- ½ teaspoon baking powder
- ⅛ teaspoon sea salt
- ¼ cup mini chocolate chips

Directions:

1. Preheat the air fryer to 165°C/330°F.
2. In a large bowl, combine the bananas, brown sugar, vanilla extract, milk, butter, and egg; set aside.
3. In a separate bowl, combine the flour, oats, baking soda, baking powder, and salt.
4. Slowly add the dry ingredients into the wet ingredients, folding in the flour mixture ⅓ cup at a time.
5. Mix in the chocolate chips and set aside.
6. Using silicone muffin liners, fill 6 muffin liners two-thirds full. Carefully place the muffin liners in the air fryer basket and bake for 20 minutes (or until the tops are browned and a toothpick inserted in the center comes out clean). Carefully remove the muffins from the basket and repeat with the remaining batter.
7. Serve warm.

Variations & Ingredients Tips:

- Use different types of chocolate chips, such as dark chocolate or white chocolate, for a variety of flavors.
- Add some chopped nuts, such as walnuts or pecans, to the muffin batter for a crunchy texture.
- For a healthier version, replace the butter with applesauce or Greek yogurt and reduce the amount of sugar.

Per Serving: Calories: 140; Total Fat: 5g; Saturated Fat: 2.5g; Cholesterol: 20mg; Sodium: 160mg; Total Carbs: 22g; Fiber: 2g; Sugars: 10g; Protein: 3g

Breakfast Chimichangas

Servings: 4 | Prep Time: 15 Minutes | Cooking Time: 8 Minutes

Ingredients:

- Four 20-cm flour tortillas
- ½ cup canned refried beans
- 1 cup scrambled eggs
- ½ cup grated cheddar or Monterey jack cheese
- 1 tablespoon vegetable oil
- 1 cup salsa

Directions:

1. Lay tortillas flat and spread 2 tbsp refried beans in the center of each.
2. Top each with ¼ cup scrambled eggs and 2 tbsp cheese.
3. Fold left side to center, then right. Fold bottom and top over and roll to seal.
4. Brush tops with oil.
5. Preheat air fryer to 205°C/400°F for 4 mins.
6. Place chimichangas seam-side down in basket and air fry 4 mins.
7. Flip and cook 2-3 more mins until golden brown.
8. Serve with salsa.

Variations & Ingredients Tips:

- Add cooked potatoes, peppers or onions to the filling.
- Use pepper jack or queso fresco cheese.
- Serve with sour cream, guacamole or hot sauce.

Per Serving: Calories: 430; Total Fat: 19g; Saturated Fat: 7g; Cholesterol: 200mg; Sodium: 1030mg; Total Carbs: 43g; Dietary Fiber: 5g; Total Sugars: 3g; Protein: 20g

Huevos Rancheros

Servings: 4 | Prep Time: 10 Minutes | Cooking Time: 45 Minutes + Cooling Time

Ingredients:

- 1 tablespoon olive oil
- 20 cherry tomatoes, halved
- 2 chopped plum tomatoes
- 59 ml tomato sauce
- 2 scallions, sliced
- 2 garlic cloves, minced
- 1 teaspoon honey
- ½ teaspoon salt
- ⅛ teaspoon cayenne pepper
- ¼ teaspoon grated nutmeg
- ¼ teaspoon paprika
- 4 eggs

Directions:

1. Preheat the air fryer to 190°C/370°F. Combine the olive oil, cherry tomatoes, plum tomatoes, tomato sauce, scallions, garlic, nutmeg, honey, salt, paprika and cayenne in an 18 cm springform pan that has been wrapped in foil to prevent leaks. Put the pan in the frying basket and Bake the mix for 15-20 minutes, stirring twice until the tomatoes are soft. Mash some of the tomatoes in the pan with a fork, then stir them into the sauce. Also, break the eggs into the sauce, then return the pan to the fryer and Bake for 2 minutes. Remove the pan from the fryer and stir the eggs into the sauce, whisking them through the sauce. Don't mix in completely. Cook for 4-8 minutes more or until the eggs are set. Let cool, then serve.

Variations & Ingredients Tips:

▶ Serve with warm corn tortillas, refried beans and sliced avocado.

▶ Top with crumbled queso fresco or cotija cheese.

▶ Add some chopped jalapeños or chipotle peppers for extra heat.

Per Serving: Calories: 164; Total Fat: 11g; Saturated Fat: 3g; Cholesterol: 186mg; Sodium: 425mg; Total Carbs: 10g; Dietary Fiber: 2g; Total Sugars: 6g; Protein: 8g

Zucchini Hash Browns

Servings: 4 | Prep Time: 8 Minutes | Cooking Time: 20 Minutes

Ingredients:

- 2 shredded zucchinis
- 2 tbsp nutritional yeast
- 1 tsp allspice
- 1 egg white

Directions:

1. Preheat air fryer to 200°C/400°F.
2. Combine zucchinis, nutritional yeast, allspice, and egg white in a bowl.
3. Make 4 patties out of the mixture.
4. Cut 4 pieces of parchment paper, put a patty on each, and fold in all sides to create a rectangle.
5. Using a spatula, flatten them and spread them out on the parchment.
6. Then unwrap each parchment and remove the hash browns onto the fryer and Air Fry for 12 minutes until golden brown and crispy, turning once.
7. Serve right away.

Variations & Ingredients Tips:

▶ Grate in carrots, onions or potatoes as well.

▶ Add shredded cheese or herbs like dill or parsley.

▶ Serve with salsa, sour cream or avocado on the side.

Per Serving: Calories: 41; Total Fat: 1g; Saturated Fat: 0g; Cholesterol: 0mg; Sodium: 34mg; Total Carbs: 6g; Dietary Fiber: 2g; Total Sugars: 3g; Protein: 4g

Hashbrown Potatoes Lyonnaise

Servings: 4 | Prep Time: 10 Minutes | Cooking Time: 33 Minutes

Ingredients:

- 1 Vidalia (or other sweet) onion, sliced
- 1 teaspoon butter, melted
- 1 teaspoon brown sugar
- 2 large russet potatoes (about 454 g), sliced 1.3 cm thick
- 1 tablespoon vegetable oil
- salt and freshly ground black pepper

Directions:

1. Preheat the air fryer to 190°C/370°F.
2. Toss the sliced onions, melted butter and brown sugar together in the air fryer basket. Air-fry for 8 minutes, shaking the basket occasionally to help the onions cook evenly.
3. While the onions are cooking, bring a 3-quart saucepan of salted water to a boil on the stovetop. Par-cook the potatoes in boiling water for 3 minutes. Drain the potatoes and pat them dry with a clean kitchen towel.
4. Add the potatoes to the onions in the air fryer basket and drizzle with vegetable oil. Toss to coat the potatoes with the oil and season with salt and freshly ground black pepper.
5. Increase the air fryer temperature to 200°C/400°F and air-fry for 22 minutes tossing the vegetables a few times during the cooking time to help the potatoes brown evenly. Season to taste again with salt and freshly ground black pepper and serve warm.

Variations & Ingredients Tips:

▶ Add some chopped bacon, ham or pancetta to the onions for a meaty flavor.

- ▶ Sprinkle with chopped fresh herbs like parsley, chives or thyme before serving.
- ▶ Top with a dollop of sour cream or crème fraîche for a creamy finish.

Per Serving: Calories: 208; Total Fat: 6g; Saturated Fat: 2g; Cholesterol: 5mg; Sodium: 64mg; Total Carbs: 35g; Dietary Fiber: 3g; Total Sugars: 4g; Protein: 4g

Crispy Chicken Cakes

Servings: 4 | Prep Time: 10 Minutes | Cooking Time: 30 Minutes

Ingredients:

- 1 peeled Granny Smith apple, chopped
- 2 scallions, chopped
- 3 tablespoons ground almonds
- 1 teaspoon garlic powder
- 1 egg white
- 2 tablespoons apple juice
- Black pepper to taste
- 450 g ground chicken

Directions:

1. Preheat air fryer to 165°C/330°F.
2. Combine the apple, scallions, almonds, garlic powder, egg white, apple juice, and pepper in a bowl. Add the ground chicken using your hands. Mix well.
3. Make 8 patties and set four in the frying basket. Air Fry for 8-12 minutes until crispy. Repeat with the remaining patties.
4. Serve hot.

Variations & Ingredients Tips:

- ▶ Use different types of ground meat, such as turkey or pork, for a variety of flavors.
- ▶ Add some grated Parmesan cheese or bread crumbs to the patty mixture for extra flavor and texture.
- ▶ Serve the chicken cakes with a side of salsa or tzatziki sauce for dipping.

Per Serving: Calories: 240; Total Fat: 14g; Saturated Fat: 3.5g; Cholesterol: 115mg; Sodium: 120mg; Total Carbs: 6g; Fiber: 1g; Sugars: 4g; Protein: 26g

Green Egg Quiche

Servings: 4 | Prep Time: 10 Minutes | Cooking Time: 30 Minutes

Ingredients:

- 1 cup broccoli florets
- 2 cups baby spinach
- 2 garlic cloves, minced
- ¼ teaspoon ground nutmeg
- 1 tablespoon olive oil
- Salt and pepper to taste
- 4 eggs
- 2 scallions, chopped
- 1 red onion, chopped
- 1 tablespoon sour cream
- 113 g grated fontina cheese

Directions:

1. Preheat air fryer to 190°C/375°F. Combine broccoli, spinach, onion, garlic, nutmeg, olive oil, and salt in a medium bowl, tossing to coat. Arrange the broccoli in a single layer in the parchment-lined frying basket and cook for 5 minutes. Remove and set to the side.
2. Use the same medium bowl to whisk eggs, salt, pepper, scallions, and sour cream. Add the roasted broccoli and 28 g fontina cheese until all ingredients are well combined. Pour the mixture into a greased baking dish and top with cheese. Bake in the air fryer for 15-18 minutes until the center is set. Serve and enjoy.

Variations & Ingredients Tips:

- ▶ Use asparagus, zucchini or bell peppers instead of broccoli.
- ▶ Swap fontina for goat cheese, feta or Parmesan.
- ▶ Serve with a simple green salad and crusty bread for a light meal.

Per Serving: Calories: 264; Total Fat: 19g; Saturated Fat: 8g; Cholesterol: 227mg; Sodium: 336mg; Total Carbs: 8g; Dietary Fiber: 2g; Total Sugars: 3g; Protein: 16g

Appetizers And Snacks

Hot Garlic Kale Chips

Servings: 6 | Prep Time: 5 Minutes | Cooking Time: 20 Minutes

Ingredients:
- 1 tbsp chili powder
- 1 tsp garlic powder
- 6 cups kale, torn
- 3 tsp olive oil
- Sea salt to taste

Directions:
1. Preheat air fryer to 200°C/390°F. Mix the garlic and chili powders. Coat the kale with olive oil, chili, and garlic powder. Put it in the frying basket and Air Fry until crispy, about 5-6 minutes, shaking the basket at around 3 minutes. Toss some sea salt on the kale chips once they are finished and serve.

Variations & Ingredients Tips:
▶ Use spinach, Swiss chard or collard greens instead of kale.
▶ Add some smoked paprika, cumin or curry powder to the seasoning mix.
▶ Sprinkle with nutritional yeast or Parmesan cheese before serving.

Per serving: Calories: 53; Total Fat: 4g; Saturated Fat: 1g; Cholesterol: 0mg; Sodium: 44mg; Total Carbs: 4g; Dietary Fiber: 1g; Total Sugars: 1g; Protein: 1g

Jalapeño & Mozzarella Stuffed Mushrooms

Servings: 4 | Prep Time: 15 Minutes | Cooking Time: 30 Minutes

Ingredients:
- 16 button mushrooms
- 1/3 cup salsa
- 3 garlic cloves, minced
- 1 onion, finely chopped
- 1 jalapeño pepper, minced
- ⅛ tsp cayenne pepper
- 3 tbsp shredded mozzarella
- 2 tsp olive oil

Directions:
1. Preheat air fryer to 177°C/350°F. Remove the stem from the mushrooms, then finely slice them. Set the caps aside. Combine the salsa, garlic, onion, jalapeño, cayenne, and mozzarella cheese in a bowl, then add the stems. Fill the mushroom caps with the mixture, making sure to overfill so the mix is coming out of the top. Drizzle with olive oil. Place the caps in the air fryer and bake for 8-12 minutes. The filling should be hot and the mushrooms soft. Serve warm.

Variations & Ingredients Tips:
▶ Use kalamata olives, black olives or a mix of different varieties.
▶ Add some grated Parmesan cheese or lemon zest to the breading.
▶ Serve as a garnish for martinis or Bloody Marys.

Per serving: Calories: 193; Total Fat: 11g; Saturated Fat: 2g; Cholesterol: 12mg; Sodium: 525mg; Total Carbs: 19g; Dietary Fiber: 2g; Total Sugars: 1g; Protein: 4g

Sweet-and-salty Pretzels

Servings: 4 | Prep Time: 5 Minutes | Cooking Time: 5 Minutes

Ingredients:
- 2 cups plain pretzel nuggets
- 1 tbsp Worcestershire sauce
- 2 tsp granulated white sugar
- 1 tsp mild smoked paprika
- ½ tsp garlic or onion powder

Directions:
1. Preheat the air fryer to 175°C/350°F. Put the pretzel nuggets, Worcestershire sauce, sugar, smoked paprika, and garlic or onion powder in a large bowl. Toss gently until the nuggets are well coated. When the machine is at temperature, pour the nuggets into the basket, spreading them into as close to a single layer as possible. Air-fry, shaking the basket three or four times to rearrange the nuggets, for 5 minutes, or until the nuggets are toasted and aromatic. Although the coating will darken, don't let it burn, especially if the machine's temperature is 180°C/360°F. Pour the nuggets onto a wire rack and gently spread them into one layer. (A rubber spatula does a good job.) Cool for 5 minutes before serving.

Variations & Ingredients Tips:
▶ Experiment with different spice blends like ranch sea-

soning, taco seasoning, or Italian herbs.
- Add a pinch of cayenne pepper or red pepper flakes for a spicy kick.
- Drizzle with melted chocolate or caramel for a sweet and salty treat.

Per Serving: Calories: 113; Total Fat: 1g; Saturated Fat: 0g; Sodium: 504mg; Total Carbohydrates: 24g; Dietary Fiber: 1g; Total Sugars: 3g; Protein: 3g

Turkey Bacon Dates

Servings: 16 | Prep Time: 15 Minutes | Cooking Time: 7 Minutes

Ingredients:
- 16 whole, pitted dates
- 16 whole almonds
- 6 to 8 strips turkey bacon

Directions:
1. Stuff each date with a whole almond. Depending on the size of your stuffed dates, cut bacon strips into halves or thirds. Each strip should be long enough to wrap completely around a date. Wrap each date in a strip of bacon with ends overlapping and secure with toothpicks. Place in air fryer basket and cook at 200°C/390°F for 7 minutes, until bacon is as crispy as you like. Drain on paper towels or wire rack. Serve hot or at room temperature.

Variations & Ingredients Tips:
- Stuff the dates with blue cheese, goat cheese, or feta instead of almonds for a creamy filling.
- Wrap the dates with prosciutto, pancetta, or regular bacon for a different flavor.
- Brush the bacon-wrapped dates with maple syrup or honey before cooking for a sweet and savory treat.

Per Serving: Calories: 54; Total Fat: 2g; Saturated Fat: 0g; Cholesterol: 3mg; Sodium: 104mg; Total Carbohydrates: 8g; Dietary Fiber: 1g; Total Sugars: 7g; Protein: 2g

Kale Chips

Servings: 2 | Prep Time: 5 Minutes | Cooking Time: 5 Minutes

Ingredients:
- 4 Medium kale leaves, about 30 g each
- 2 teaspoons Olive oil
- 2 teaspoons Regular or low-sodium soy sauce or gluten-free tamari sauce

Directions:
1. Preheat the air fryer to 200°C/400°F.
2. Cut the stems from the leaves (all the stems, all the way up the leaf). Tear each leaf into three pieces. Put them in a large bowl.
3. Add the olive oil and soy or tamari sauce. Toss well to coat. You can even gently rub the leaves along the side of the bowl to get the liquids to stick to them.
4. When the machine is at temperature, put the leaf pieces in the basket in one layer. Air-fry for 5 minutes, turning and rearranging with kitchen tongs once halfway through, until the chips are dried out and crunchy. Watch carefully so they don't turn dark brown at the edges.
5. Gently pour the contents of the basket onto a wire rack. Cool for at least 5 minutes before serving. The chips can keep for up to 8 hours uncovered on the rack (provided it's not a humid day).

Variations & Ingredients Tips:
- Use collard greens, Swiss chard or spinach instead of kale.
- Season with garlic powder, smoked paprika or nutritional yeast.
- Store leftovers in an airtight container at room temperature for up to 3 days.

Per serving: Calories: 75; Total Fat: 5g; Saturated Fat: 1g; Cholesterol: 0mg; Sodium: 237mg; Total Carbs: 6g; Dietary Fiber: 2g; Total Sugars: 1g; Protein: 3g

Poppy Seed Mini Hot Dog Rolls

Servings: 4 | Prep Time: 10 Minutes | Cooking Time: 25 Minutes

Ingredients:
- 8 small mini hot dogs
- 8 pastry dough sheets
- 1 tbsp vegetable oil
- 1 tbsp poppy seeds

Directions:
1. Preheat the air fryer to 175°C/350°F. Roll the mini hot dogs into a pastry dough sheet, wrapping them snugly. Brush the rolls with vegetable oil on all sides. Arrange them on the frying basket and sprinkle poppy seeds on top. Bake for 15 minutes until the pastry crust is golden brown. Serve.

Variations & Ingredients Tips:
- Use different types of sausages like bratwurst, Italian

sausage, or chorizo for variety.
- ▶ Brush the rolls with beaten egg instead of oil for a shinier, golden finish.
- ▶ Serve with mustard, ketchup, or your favorite dipping sauce.

Per serving: Calories: 298; Total Fat: 23g; Saturated Fat: 5g; Cholesterol: 15mg; Sodium: 417mg; Total Carbs: 17g; Dietary Fiber: 1g; Total Sugars: 1g; Protein: 6g

Garam Masala Cauliflower Pakoras

Servings: 4 | Prep Time: 15 Minutes | Cooking Time: 30 Minutes

Ingredients:
- ½ cup chickpea flour
- 1 tbsp cornstarch
- Salt to taste
- 2 tsp cumin powder
- ½ tsp coriander powder
- ½ tsp turmeric
- 1 tsp garam masala
- ⅛ tsp baking soda
- ⅛ tsp cayenne powder
- 1 ½ cups minced onion
- ½ cup chopped cilantro
- ½ cup chopped cauliflower
- ¼ cup lime juice

Directions:
1. Preheat air fryer to 175°C/350°F. Combine the flour, cornstarch, salt, cumin, coriander, turmeric, garam masala, baking soda, and cayenne in a bowl. Stir well. Mix in the onion, cilantro, cauliflower, and lime juice. Using your hands, stir the mix, massaging the flour and spices into the vegetables. Form the mixture into balls and place them in the greased frying basket. Spray the tops of the pakoras in the air fryer with oil and Air Fry for 15-18 minutes, turning once until browned and crispy. Serve hot.

Variations & Ingredients Tips:
- ▶ Add some shredded potatoes or carrots to the vegetable mixture.
- ▶ Substitute broccoli, zucchini or bell peppers for the cauliflower.
- ▶ Serve with tamarind chutney, mint-cilantro chutney or raita yogurt sauce.

Per serving: Calories: 142; Total Fat: 2g; Saturated Fat: 0g; Cholesterol: 0mg; Sodium: 329mg; Total Carbs: 27g; Dietary Fiber: 5g; Total Sugars: 5g; Protein: 6g

Crispy Curried Sweet Potato Fries

Servings: 4 | Prep Time: 10 Minutes | Cooking Time: 20 Minutes

Ingredients:
- ½ cup sour cream
- ½ cup peach chutney
- 3 tsp curry powder
- 2 sweet potatoes, julienned
- 1 tbsp olive oil
- Salt and pepper to taste

Directions:
1. Preheat air fryer to 200°C/390°F. Mix together sour cream, peach chutney, and 1 ½ tsp curry powder in a small bowl. Set aside. In a medium bowl, add sweet potatoes, olive oil, the rest of the curry powder, salt, and pepper. Toss to coat. Place the potatoes in the frying basket. Bake for about 6 minutes, then shake the basket once. Cook for an additional 4-6 minutes or until the potatoes are golden and crispy. Serve the fries hot in a basket along with the chutney sauce for dipping.

Variations & Ingredients Tips:
- ▶ Use russet potatoes or carrots instead of sweet potatoes.
- ▶ Add some garlic powder or garam masala to the spice mixture.
- ▶ Serve with mango chutney or raita yogurt sauce for dipping.

Per serving: Calories: 265; Total Fat: 11g; Saturated Fat: 4g; Cholesterol: 15mg; Sodium: 128mg; Total Carbs: 41g; Dietary Fiber: 4g; Total Sugars: 22g; Protein: 3g

Roasted Red Pepper Dip

Servings: 2 | Prep Time: 10 Minutes | Cooking Time: 15 Minutes

Ingredients:
- 2 medium-size red bell peppers
- 425 g canned white beans, drained and rinsed
- 1 tbsp fresh oregano leaves, packed
- 3 tbsp olive oil
- 1 tbsp lemon juice
- ½ tsp table salt
- ½ tsp ground black pepper

Directions:
1. Preheat the air fryer to 200°C/400°F. Set the peppers in the basket and air-fry undisturbed for 15 minutes, un-

til blistered and even blackened. Use kitchen tongs to transfer the peppers to a zip-closed plastic bag or small bowl. Seal the bag or cover the bowl with plastic wrap. Set aside for 20 minutes. Peel each pepper, then stem it, cut it in half, and remove all its seeds and their white membranes. Set the pieces of the pepper in a food processor. Add the beans, oregano, olive oil, lemon juice, salt, and pepper. Cover and process until smooth, stopping the machine at least once to scrape down the inside of the canister. Scrape the dip into a bowl and serve warm, or cover and refrigerate for up to 3 days (although the dip tastes best if it's allowed to come back to room temperature).

Variations & Ingredients Tips:

▶ Roast a head of garlic along with the peppers and add the cloves to the dip for a deeper flavor.

▶ Use cannellini beans, chickpeas, or black beans instead of white beans for a different taste and texture.

▶ Add smoked paprika, cumin, or hot sauce for a smoky or spicy kick.

Per serving: Calories: 437; Total Fat: 22g; Saturated Fat: 3g; Cholesterol: 0mg; Sodium: 886mg; Total Carbs: 47g; Dietary Fiber: 12g; Total Sugars: 3g; Protein: 17g

Fried Olives

Servings: 5 | Prep Time: 15 Minutes | Cooking Time: 10 Minutes

Ingredients:

- ⅓ cup All-purpose flour or tapioca flour
- 1 Large egg white(s)
- 1 tablespoon Brine from the olive jar
- ⅔ cup Plain dried bread crumbs (gluten-free, if a concern)
- 15 Large pimiento-stuffed green olives
- Olive oil spray

Directions:

1. Preheat the air fryer to 200°C/400°F.

2. Pour the flour in a medium-size zip-closed plastic bag. Whisk the egg white and pickle brine in a medium bowl until foamy. Spread out the bread crumbs on a dinner plate.

3. Pour all the olives into the bag with the flour, seal, and shake to coat the olives. Remove a couple of olives, shake off any excess flour, and drop them into the egg white mixture. Toss gently but well to coat. Pick them up one at a time and roll each in the bread crumbs until well coated on all sides, even the ends. Set them aside

on a cutting board as you finish the rest. When done coat the olives with olive oil spray on all sides.

4. Place the olives in the basket in one layer. Air-fry for 8 minutes, gently shaking the basket once halfway through the cooking process to rearrange the olives, until lightly browned.

5. Gently pour the olives onto a wire rack and cool for at least 10 minutes before serving. Once cooled, the olives may be stored in a sealed container in the fridge for up to 2 days. To rewarm them, set them in the basket of a heated 200°C/400°F air fryer undisturbed for 2 minutes.

Variations & Ingredients Tips:

▶ Use blue cheese, feta or almond-stuffed olives for different fillings.

▶ Add some smoked paprika, garlic powder or dried herbs to the breading.

▶ Serve as a garnish for martinis or bloody marys.

Per serving: Calories: 120; Total Fat: 8g; Saturated Fat: 1g; Cholesterol: 0mg; Sodium: 516mg; Total Carbs: 9g; Dietary Fiber: 1g; Total Sugars: 1g; Protein: 2g

Fried Peaches

Servings: 4 | Prep Time: 15 Minutes | Cooking Time: 8 Minutes

Ingredients:

- 2 egg whites
- 1 tablespoon water
- ¼ cup sliced almonds
- 2 tablespoons brown sugar
- ½ teaspoon almond extract
- 1 cup crisp rice cereal
- 2 medium, very firm peaches, peeled and pitted
- ¼ cup cornstarch
- oil for misting or cooking spray

Directions:

1. Preheat air fryer to 200°C/390°F.

2. Beat together egg whites and water in a shallow dish.

3. In a food processor, combine the almonds, brown sugar, and almond extract. Process until ingredients combine well and the nuts are finely chopped.

4. Add cereal and pulse just until cereal crushes. Pour crumb mixture into a shallow dish or onto a plate.

5. Cut each peach into eighths and place in a plastic bag or container with lid. Add cornstarch, seal, and shake to coat.

6. Remove peach slices from bag or container, tapping them hard to shake off the excess cornstarch. Dip in egg

wash and roll in crumbs. Spray with oil.

7. Place in air fryer basket and cook for 5 minutes. Shake basket, separate any that have stuck together, and spritz a little oil on any spots that aren't browning.

8. Cook for 3 minutes longer, until golden brown and crispy.

Variations & Ingredients Tips:

- Use nectarines, apricots or plums instead of peaches.
- Add some cinnamon, nutmeg or cardamom to the crumb mixture.
- Serve with vanilla ice cream, whipped cream or caramel sauce for dipping.

Per serving: Calories: 172; Total Fat: 5g; Saturated Fat: 1g; Cholesterol: 0mg; Sodium: 76mg; Total Carbs: 30g; Dietary Fiber: 3g; Total Sugars: 17g; Protein: 4g

Shrimp Pirogues

Servings: 8 | Prep Time: 20 Minutes | Cooking Time: 5 Minutes

Ingredients:

- 340 g small, peeled, and deveined raw shrimp
- 85 g cream cheese, room temperature
- 2 tablespoons plain yogurt
- 1 teaspoon lemon juice
- 1 teaspoon dried dill weed, crushed
- Salt
- 4 small hothouse cucumbers, each approximately 15 cm long

Directions:

1. Pour 4 tablespoons water in bottom of air fryer drawer.
2. Place shrimp in air fryer basket in single layer and cook at 200°C/390°F for 5 minutes, just until done. Watch carefully because shrimp cooks quickly, and overcooking makes it tough.
3. Chop shrimp into small pieces, no larger than 1.25 cm. Refrigerate while mixing the remaining ingredients.
4. With a fork, mash and whip the cream cheese until smooth.
5. Stir in the yogurt and beat until smooth. Stir in lemon juice, dill weed, and chopped shrimp.
6. Taste for seasoning. If needed, add ¼ to ½ teaspoon salt to suit your taste.
7. Store in refrigerator until serving time.
8. When ready to serve, wash and dry cucumbers and split them lengthwise. Scoop out the seeds and turn cucumbers upside down on paper towels to drain for 10 minutes.
9. Just before filling, wipe centers of cucumbers dry. Spoon the shrimp mixture into the pirogues and cut in half crosswise. Serve immediately.

Variations & Ingredients Tips:

- Replace the plain yogurt with sour cream or mayonnaise for a richer flavor.
- Add minced garlic or finely chopped red onion to the filling for extra flavor.
- Use zucchini or yellow squash instead of cucumbers for a different vegetable base.

Per Serving: Calories: 75; Total Fat: 5g; Saturated Fat: 3g; Cholesterol: 60mg; Sodium: 115mg; Total Carbs: 2g; Fiber: 0g; Sugars: 1g; Protein: 6g

Roasted Tomatillo Salsa

Servings: 4 | Prep Time: 10 Minutes | Cooking Time: 35 Minutes + Cooling Time

Ingredients:

- 2 tbsp olive oil
- 1 serrano pepper
- 1 jalapeño pepper
- ¼ white onion
- 2 garlic cloves
- 340 g tomatillos
- 3 tbsp chopped cilantro
- ¼ tsp sugar
- Salt to taste

Directions:

1. Preheat air fryer to 200°C/400°F. Lightly drizzle the serrano, jalapeño, onion and garlic with some olive oil. Bake in the air fryer for 14 minutes, flipping them once until charred. Remove the peppers to a foil, wrap and let cool for 10 minutes. Put the rest of the veggies into a food processor. Lightly brush the tomatillos with the remaining olive oil. Cook in the air fryer for 10 minutes, flipping the tomatillos once until charred. Transfer the tomatillos to your food processor. Unwrap the peppers. Peel off the skin and remove all of the seeds. Transfer to the food processor. Also, add cilantro, sugar, and salt. Pulse until coarsely chopped. Slowly add 5-6 tbsp of water until smooth and pureed. Serve.

Variations & Ingredients Tips:

- Add lime juice, cumin, or oregano for extra flavor.
- Roast a few cloves of garlic along with the vegetables for a deeper, richer taste.
- Adjust the amount of serrano and jalapeño peppers to make the salsa milder or spicier.

Per serving: Calories: 101; Total Fat: 7g; Saturated Fat: 1g; Cholesterol: 0mg; Sodium: 9mg; Total Carbs: 9g; Dietary Fiber: 2g; Total Sugars: 5g; Protein: 1g

Rosemary Garlic Goat Cheese

Servings: 4 | Prep Time: 10 Minutes | Cooking Time: 20 Minutes

Ingredients:

- 2 peeled garlic cloves roasted
- 340 g goat cheese
- ½ cup grated Parmesan
- 1 egg, beaten
- 1 tbsp olive oil
- 1 tbsp apple cider vinegar
- Salt and pepper to taste
- 1 tsp chopped rosemary

Directions:

1. Preheat air fryer to 175°C/350°F. Carefully squeeze the garl0ic into a bowl and mash it with a fork until a paste is formed. Stir in goat cheese, Parmesan, egg, olive oil, vinegar, salt, black pepper, and rosemary. Spoon the mixture into a baking dish, and place the dish in the frying basket. Air fry for 7 minutes. Serve warm.

Variations & Ingredients Tips:

▶ Use different herbs like thyme, basil, or oregano instead of rosemary.

▶ Add sun-dried tomatoes, olives, or roasted red peppers for a Mediterranean twist.

▶ Serve with crostini, crackers, or sliced baguette for spreading.

Per serving: Calories: 273; Total Fat: 22g; Saturated Fat: 13g; Cholesterol: 78mg; Sodium: 441mg; Total Carbs: 2g; Dietary Fiber: 0g; Total Sugars: 1g; Protein: 17g

Avocado Fries

Servings: 4 | Prep Time: 15 Minutes | Cooking Time: 10 Minutes

Ingredients:

- 1 egg
- 1 tablespoon lime juice
- ⅛ teaspoon hot sauce
- 2 tablespoons flour
- ¾ cup panko breadcrumbs
- ¼ cup cornmeal
- ¼ teaspoon salt
- 1 large avocado
- oil for misting or cooking spray

Directions:

1. In a small bowl, whisk together the egg, lime juice, and hot sauce.
2. Place flour on a sheet of wax paper.
3. Mix panko, cornmeal, and salt and place on another sheet of wax paper.
4. Split avocado in half and remove pit. Peel or use a spoon to lift avocado halves from the skin.
5. Cut avocado lengthwise into 13 mm slices. Dip each in flour, then egg wash, then roll in panko mixture.
6. Mist with oil or cooking spray and cook at 200°C/390°F for 10 minutes, until crust is brown and crispy.

Variations & Ingredients Tips:

▶ Use seasoned breadcrumbs for extra flavor.

▶ Substitute the egg with milk for a vegan version.

▶ Sprinkle with chili-lime seasoning after cooking.

Per serving: Calories: 208; Total Fat: 13g; Saturated Fat: 2g; Cholesterol: 47mg; Sodium: 292mg; Total Carbs: 20g; Dietary Fiber: 5g; Total Sugars: 2g; Protein: 5g

Zucchini Fries With Roasted Garlic Aïoli

Servings: 4 | Prep Time: 20 Minutes | Cooking Time: 12 Minutes

Ingredients:

- Roasted Garlic Aïoli:
- 1 tsp roasted garlic
- ½ cup mayonnaise
- 2 tbsp olive oil
- juice of ½ lemon
- salt and pepper
- Zucchini Fries:
- ½ cup flour
- 2 eggs, beaten
- 1 cup seasoned breadcrumbs
- salt and pepper
- 1 large zucchini, cut into 1.3-cm sticks
- olive oil in a spray bottle, can or mister

Directions:

1. To make the aïoli, combine the roasted garlic, mayonnaise, olive oil and lemon juice in a bowl and whisk well. Season the aïoli with salt and pepper to taste. Prepare the zucchini fries. Create a dredging station with three shallow dishes. Place the flour in the first shallow dish and season well with salt and freshly ground black pepper. Put the beaten eggs in the second shallow dish. In the third shallow dish, combine the breadcrumbs, salt and pepper. Dredge the zucchini sticks, coating with flour first, then dipping them into the eggs to coat, and finally tossing in breadcrumbs. Shake the dish with the breadcrumbs and pat the crumbs onto the zucchini

sticks gently with your hands so they stick evenly. Place the zucchini fries on a flat surface and let them sit at least 10 minutes before air-frying to let them dry out a little. Preheat the air fryer to 200°C/400°F. Spray the zucchini sticks with olive oil, and place them into the air fryer basket. You can air-fry the zucchini in two layers, placing the second layer in the opposite direction to the first. Air-fry for 12 minutes turning and rotating the fries halfway through the cooking time. Spray with additional oil when you turn them over. Serve zucchini fries warm with the roasted garlic aïoli.

Variations & Ingredients Tips:

- ▶ Add grated Parmesan cheese, herbs, or spices to the breadcrumb mixture for extra flavor.
- ▶ Use panko breadcrumbs for an extra crispy coating.
- ▶ Serve with marinara sauce, ranch dressing, or spicy mayo for dipping variety.

Per Serving: Calories: 341; Total Fat: 24g; Saturated Fat: 4g; Cholesterol: 96mg; Sodium: 465mg; Total Carbohydrates: 25g; Dietary Fiber: 2g; Total Sugars: 3g; Protein: 8g

Thick-crust Pepperoni Pizza

Servings: 2 | Prep Time: 10 Minutes | Cooking Time: 10 Minutes

Ingredients:

- 285 g purchased fresh pizza dough (not a pre-baked crust)
- Olive oil spray
- ¼ cup purchased pizza sauce
- 10 slices sliced pepperoni
- 85 g purchased shredded Italian 3- or 4-cheese blend

Directions:

1. Preheat the air fryer to 200°C/400°F. Generously coat the inside of a 15-cm round cake pan for a small air fryer, an 18-cm round cake pan for a medium air fryer, or a 20-cm round cake pan for a large model with olive oil spray. Set the dough in the pan and press it to fill the bottom in an even, thick layer. Spread the sauce over the dough, then top with the pepperoni and cheese. When the machine is at temperature, set the pan in the basket and air-fry undisturbed for 10 minutes, or until puffed, brown, and bubbling. Use kitchen tongs to transfer the cake pan to a wire rack. Cool for only a minute or so. Use a spatula to loosen the pizza from the pan and lift it out and onto the rack. Continue cooling for a few minutes before cutting into wedges to serve.

Variations & Ingredients Tips:

- ▶ Add your favorite pizza toppings like sausage, mushrooms, onions, or bell peppers.
- ▶ Brush the crust with garlic butter or sprinkle with Italian seasoning for extra flavor.
- ▶ Use a pre-made pizza crust or flatbread for a quicker and easier version.

Per Serving: Calories: 528; Total Fat: 22g; Saturated Fat: 8g; Cholesterol: 40mg; Sodium: 1274mg; Total Carbohydrates: 62g; Dietary Fiber: 3g; Total Sugars: 5g; Protein: 21g

Carrot Chips

Servings: 6 | Prep Time: 10 Minutes | Cooking Time: 38 Minutes

Ingredients:

- 570 g Frozen sliced carrots, preferably crinkle cut
- Vegetable oil spray
- 1½ teaspoons Table salt

Directions:

1. Preheat the air fryer to 200°C/400°F.
2. Place the carrots in a bowl. Generously coat them with vegetable oil spray, then toss well, making sure none are stuck together. Spray again, add the salt, and toss well until all the carrots are coated.
3. When the machine is at temperature, pour the carrots into the basket. Air-fry for 38 minutes, shaking the basket at the 10-, 15-, and 20-minute marks, then about every 3 minutes thereafter, until the chips are crisp and golden brown.
4. Pour the carrots onto a wire rack in one layer. Cool for at least 5 minutes before serving.

Variations & Ingredients Tips:

- ▶ Toss the cooked chips with some grated Parmesan or nutritional yeast.
- ▶ Experiment with different seasonings like ranch powder or everything bagel seasoning.
- ▶ Dip the chips in spinach artichoke dip or french onion dip.

Per serving: Calories: 74; Total Fat: 0g; Saturated Fat: 0g; Cholesterol: 0mg; Sodium: 716mg; Total Carbs: 16g; Dietary Fiber: 4g; Total Sugars: 8g; Protein: 1g | Prep Time: 5 minutes

Buffalo Bites

Servings: 16 | Prep Time: 15 Minutes | Cooking Time: 12 Minutes

Ingredients:
- 450 g ground chicken
- 8 tablespoons buffalo wing sauce
- 60 g Gruyère cheese, cut into 16 cubes
- 1 tablespoon maple syrup

Directions:
1. Mix 4 tablespoons buffalo wing sauce into all the ground chicken.
2. Shape chicken into a log and divide into 16 equal portions.
3. With slightly damp hands, mold each chicken portion around a cube of cheese and shape into a firm ball. When you have shaped 8 meatballs, place them in air fryer basket.
4. Cook at 200°C/390°F for approximately 5 minutes. Shake basket, reduce temperature to 180°C/360°F, and cook for 5 minutes longer.
5. While the first batch is cooking, shape remaining chicken and cheese into 8 more meatballs.
6. Repeat step 4 to cook second batch of meatballs.
7. In a medium bowl, mix the remaining 4 tablespoons of buffalo wing sauce with the maple syrup. Add all the cooked meatballs and toss to coat.
8. Place meatballs back into air fryer basket and cook at 200°C/390°F for 2 minutes to set the glaze. Skewer each with a toothpick and serve.

Variations & Ingredients Tips:
- Use blue cheese instead of Gruyère for a classic buffalo flavor.
- Add some chopped celery or carrots to the chicken mixture for extra crunch.
- Serve with ranch or blue cheese dressing for dipping.

Per serving: Calories: 88; Total Fat: 5g; Saturated Fat: 2g; Cholesterol: 39mg; Sodium: 300mg; Total Carbs: 2g; Dietary Fiber: 0g; Total Sugars: 1g; Protein: 8g

Ranch Chips

Servings: 2 | Prep Time: 40 Minutes | Cooking Time: 30 Minutes

Ingredients:
- 1 tsp dry ranch seasoning
- Salt and pepper to taste
- 2 cups sliced potatoes
- 2 tsp olive oil
- ¼ cup white wine vinegar

Directions:
1. Preheat air fryer at 200°C/400°F. In a bowl, combine ranch mix, salt, and pepper. Reserve ½ tsp for garnish. In another bowl, mix sliced fingerling potatoes with the vinegar and stir around. Let soak in the vinegar water for at least thirty minutes then drain the potatoes and pat them dry. Place potato chips and spread with olive oil until coated. Sprinkle with the ranch mixture and toss to coat. Place potato chips in the frying basket and air fry for 16 minutes, shaking 4 times. Transfer it into a bowl. Sprinkle with the reserved mixture and let sit for 15 minutes. Serve immediately.

Variations & Ingredients Tips:
- Try different seasoning blends like BBQ, sour cream and onion, or salt and vinegar.
- Use sweet potatoes or other root vegetables for a colorful twist.
- For a healthier option, use less oil and more vinegar for tangier chips.

Per serving: Calories: 188; Total Fat: 7g; Saturated Fat: 1g; Cholesterol: 0mg; Sodium: 323mg; Total Carbs: 29g; Dietary Fiber: 3g; Total Sugars: 2g; Protein: 3g

Poultry Recipes

Chicken Souvlaki Gyros

Servings: 4 | Prep Time: 15 Minutes (plus 2 Hours Marinating Time) | Cooking Time: 18 Minutes

Ingredients:

- ¼ cup extra-virgin olive oil
- 1 clove garlic, crushed
- 1 tablespoon Italian seasoning
- ½ teaspoon paprika
- ½ lemon, sliced
- ¼ teaspoon salt
- 454 grams boneless, skinless chicken breasts
- 4 whole-grain pita breads
- 1 cup shredded lettuce
- ½ cup chopped tomatoes
- ¼ cup chopped red onion
- ¼ cup cucumber yogurt sauce

Directions:

1. In a large resealable plastic bag, combine the olive oil, garlic, Italian seasoning, paprika, lemon, and salt. Add the chicken to the bag and secure shut. Vigorously shake until all the ingredients are combined. Set in the fridge for 2 hours to marinate.
2. When ready to cook, preheat the air fryer to 180°C/360°F.
3. Liberally spray the air fryer basket with olive oil mist. Remove the chicken from the bag and discard the leftover marinade. Place the chicken into the air fryer basket, allowing enough room between the chicken breasts to flip.
4. Cook for 10 minutes, flip, and cook another 8 minutes.
5. Remove the chicken from the air fryer basket when it has cooked (or the internal temperature of the chicken reaches 74°C/165°F). Let rest 5 minutes. Then thinly slice the chicken into strips.
6. Assemble the gyros by placing the pita bread on a flat surface and topping with chicken, lettuce, tomatoes, onion, and a drizzle of yogurt sauce.
7. Serve warm.

Variations & Ingredients Tips:

- Use Greek seasoning or za'atar spice blend instead of Italian seasoning.
- Add crumbled feta cheese or sliced Kalamata olives as toppings.
- Serve with a side of Greek salad or lemon-roasted potatoes.

Per Serving: Calories: 430; Total Fat: 19g; Saturated Fat: 3g; Sodium: 480mg; Total Carbohydrates: 30g; Dietary Fiber: 5g; Total Sugars: 4g; Protein: 37g

Yogurt-marinated Chicken Legs

Servings: 4 | Prep Time: 10 Minutes (plus Marinating Time) | Cooking Time: 50 Minutes

Ingredients:

- 1 cup Greek yogurt
- 1 tbsp Dijon mustard
- 1 tsp smoked paprika
- 1 tbsp crushed red pepper
- 1 tsp garlic powder
- 1 tsp dried oregano
- 1 tsp dried thyme
- 1 teaspoon ground cumin
- 1/4 cup lemon juice
- Salt and pepper to taste
- 680g chicken legs
- 3 tbsp butter, melted

Directions:

1. Combine all ingredients, except chicken and butter, in a bowl. Fold in chicken legs and toss until coated. Let sit covered in the fridge for 60 minutes up to overnight.
2. Preheat air fryer at 190°C/375°F. Shake excess marinade from chicken; place them in the greased frying basket and Air Fry for 18 minutes, brush melted butter and flip once.
3. Let chill for 5 minutes before serving.

Variations & Ingredients Tips:

- Use buttermilk or coconut milk instead of yogurt for a different flavor profile.
- Add grated ginger or turmeric to the marinade for an Indian twist.
- Serve with mint-cucumber raita or mango chutney on the side.

Per serving: Calories: 470; Total Fat: 30g; Saturated Fat: 12g; Cholesterol: 245mg; Sodium: 510mg; Total Carbs: 5g; Dietary Fiber: 1g; Total Sugars: 3g; Protein: 45g

Philly Chicken Cheesesteak Stromboli

Servings: 2 | Prep Time: 30 Minutes | Cooking Time: 28 Minutes

Ingredients:

29

- ½ onion, sliced
- 1 teaspoon vegetable oil
- 2 boneless, skinless chicken breasts, partially frozen and sliced very thin on the bias (about 450g)
- 1 tablespoon Worcestershire sauce
- Salt and freshly ground black pepper
- ½ recipe of Blue Jean Chef pizza dough, or 400g of store-bought pizza dough
- 1½ cups grated Cheddar cheese
- ½ cup Cheese Whiz® (or other jarred cheese sauce), warmed gently in the microwave
- Tomato ketchup for serving

Directions:

1. Preheat the air fryer to 200°C/400°F.
2. Toss the sliced onion with oil and air-fry for 8 minutes, stirring halfway through the cooking time. Add the sliced chicken and Worcestershire sauce to the air fryer basket, and toss to evenly distribute the ingredients. Season the mixture with salt and freshly ground black pepper and air-fry for 8 minutes, stirring a couple of times during the cooking process. Remove the chicken and onion from the air fryer and let the mixture cool a little.
3. On a lightly floured surface, roll or press the pizza dough out into a 33-cm by 28-cm rectangle, with the long side closest to you. Sprinkle half of the Cheddar cheese over the dough leaving an empty 2.5-cm border from the edge farthest away from you. Top the cheese with the chicken and onion mixture, spreading it out evenly. Drizzle the cheese sauce over the meat and sprinkle the remaining Cheddar cheese on top.
4. Start rolling the stromboli away from you and toward the empty border. Make sure the filling stays tightly tucked inside the roll. Finally, tuck the ends of the dough in and pinch the seam shut. Place the seam side down and shape the Stromboli into a U-shape to fit in the air-fry basket. Cut 4 small slits with the tip of a sharp knife evenly in the top of the dough and lightly brush the stromboli with a little oil.
5. Preheat the air fryer to 190°C/370°F.
6. Spray or brush the air fryer basket with oil and transfer the U-shaped stromboli to the air fryer basket. Air-fry for 12 minutes, turning the stromboli over halfway through the cooking time. (Use a plate to invert the stromboli out of the air fryer basket and then slide it back into the basket off the plate.)
7. To remove, carefully flip stromboli over onto a cutting board. Let it rest for a couple of minutes before serving. Slice the stromboli into 5-cm pieces and serve with ketchup for dipping, if desired.

Variations & Ingredients Tips:

▶ Use thinly sliced roast beef instead of chicken for a classic Philly cheesesteak.

▶ Add sautéed bell peppers and mushrooms to the filling.

▶ Brush the stromboli with garlic butter before air frying for extra flavor.

Per serving: Calories: 970; Total Fat: 51g; Saturated Fat: 24g; Cholesterol: 210mg; Sodium: 1740mg; Total Carbs: 61g; Dietary Fiber: 3g; Total Sugars: 6g; Protein: 72g

Jerk Chicken Drumsticks

Servings: 2 | Prep Time: 10 Minutes (plus Marinating Time) | Cooking Time: 20 Minutes

Ingredients:

- 1 or 2 cloves garlic
- 2.5-cm of fresh ginger
- 2 serrano peppers, (with seeds if you like it spicy, seeds removed for less heat)
- 1 teaspoon ground allspice
- 1 teaspoon ground nutmeg
- 1 teaspoon chili powder
- 1/2 teaspoon dried thyme
- 1/2 teaspoon ground cinnamon
- 1/2 teaspoon paprika
- 1 tablespoon brown sugar
- 1 teaspoon soy sauce
- 2 tablespoons vegetable oil
- 6 skinless chicken drumsticks

Directions:

1. Combine all the ingredients except the chicken in a small chopper or blender and blend to a paste. Make slashes into the meat of the chicken drumsticks and rub the spice blend all over the chicken (a pair of plastic gloves makes this really easy). Transfer the rubbed chicken to a non-reactive covered container and let the chicken marinate for at least 30 minutes or overnight in the refrigerator.
2. Preheat the air fryer to 200°C/400°F.
3. Transfer the drumsticks to the air fryer basket. Air-fry for 10 minutes. Turn the drumsticks over and air-fry for another 10 minutes.
4. Serve warm with some rice and vegetables or a green salad.

Variations & Ingredients Tips:

▶ Use bone-in chicken thighs or wings instead of drumsticks.

▶ Add a squeeze of lime juice to the marinade for acidity.

▶ Serve with mango salsa or pineapple chutney.

Per serving: Calories: 440; Total Fat: 28g; Saturated Fat: 6g; Cholesterol: 215mg; Sodium: 570mg; Total Carbs: 9g; Dietary Fiber: 1g; Total Sugars: 6g; Protein: 41g

Turkey-hummus Wraps

Servings: 4 | Prep Time: 10 Minutes | Cooking Time: 7 Minutes Per Batch

Ingredients:

- 4 large whole wheat wraps
- ½ cup hummus
- 16 thin slices deli turkey
- 8 slices provolone cheese
- 1 cup fresh baby spinach (or more to taste)

Directions:

1. To assemble, place 2 tablespoons of hummus on each wrap and spread to within about 25 cm from edges. Top with 4 slices of turkey and 2 slices of provolone. Finish with 1/4 cup of baby spinach—or pile on as much as you like.
2. Roll up each wrap. You don't need to fold or seal the ends.
3. Place 2 wraps in air fryer basket, seam side down.
4. Cook at 180°C/360°F for 4 minutes to warm filling and melt cheese. If you like, you can continue cooking for 3 more minutes, until the wrap is slightly crispy.
5. Repeat step 4 to cook remaining wraps.

Variations & Ingredients Tips:

- ▶ Use flavored hummus like roasted red pepper or garlic.
- ▶ Add sliced cucumbers, tomatoes or roasted veggies.
- ▶ Make it vegetarian by using sliced feta or fresh mozzarella instead of turkey.

Per serving: Calories: 420; Total Fat: 18g; Saturated Fat: 8g; Cholesterol: 55mg; Sodium: 1260mg; Total Carbs: 42g; Dietary Fiber: 5g; Total Sugars: 6g; Protein: 28g

Southern-fried Chicken Livers

Servings: 4 | Prep Time: 20 Minutes | Cooking Time: 12 Minutes

Ingredients:

- 2 eggs
- 2 tablespoons water
- ¾ cup flour
- 1½ cups panko breadcrumbs
- ½ cup plain breadcrumbs
- 1 teaspoon salt
- ½ teaspoon black pepper
- 567 grams chicken livers, salted to taste
- oil for misting or cooking spray

Directions:

1. Beat together eggs and water in a shallow dish. Place the flour in a separate shallow dish.
2. In the bowl of a food processor, combine the panko, plain breadcrumbs, salt, and pepper. Process until well mixed and panko crumbs are finely crushed. Place crumbs in a third shallow dish.
3. Dip livers in flour, then egg wash, and then roll in panko mixture to coat well with crumbs.
4. Spray both sides of livers with oil or cooking spray. Cooking in two batches, place livers in air fryer basket in single layer.
5. Cook at 200°C/390°F for 7 minutes. Spray livers, turn over, and spray again. Cook for 5 more minutes, until done inside and coating is golden brown.
6. Repeat to cook remaining livers.

Variations & Ingredients Tips:

- ▶ Soak the chicken livers in milk or buttermilk for 30 minutes before coating for a milder flavor.
- ▶ Add garlic powder, onion powder, or dried herbs to the breading mixture for extra seasoning.
- ▶ Serve with hot sauce, ranch dressing, or honey mustard for dipping.

Per Serving: Calories: 430; Total Fat: 17g; Saturated Fat: 4.5g; Sodium: 980mg; Total Carbohydrates: 35g; Dietary Fiber: 2g; Total Sugars: 2g; Protein: 35g

Japanese-style Turkey Meatballs

Servings: 4 | Prep Time: 15 Minutes | Cooking Time: 25 Minutes

Ingredients:

- 600g ground turkey
- 1/4 cup panko bread crumbs
- 4 chopped scallions
- 1/4 cup chopped cilantro
- 1 egg
- 1 tbsp grated ginger
- 1 garlic clove, minced
- 3 tbsp shoyu
- 2 tsp toasted sesame oil
- 3/4 tsp salt
- 2 tbsp oyster sauce
- 2 tbsp fresh orange juice

Directions:

1. Add ground turkey, panko, 3 scallions, cilantro, egg, ginger, garlic, 1 tbsp of shoyu sauce, sesame oil, and salt in a bowl. Mix with hands until combined.
2. Divide the mixture into 12 equal parts and roll into

balls.

3. Preheat air fryer to 190°C/380°F. Place the meatballs in the greased frying basket. Bake for about 9-11 minutes, flipping once until browned and cooked through. Repeat for all meatballs.
4. In a small saucepan over medium heat, add oyster sauce, orange juice and remaining shoyu sauce. Bring to a boil, then reduce the heat to low. Cook until the sauce is slightly reduced, 3 minutes.
5. Serve the meatballs with the oyster sauce drizzled over them and topped with the remaining scallions.

Variations & Ingredients Tips:

- ▶ Use ground chicken or pork instead of turkey.
- ▶ Add some Sriracha to the sauce for heat.
- ▶ Serve as an appetizer with toothpicks or in a bahn mi sandwich.

Per serving: Calories: 330; Total Fat: 17g; Saturated Fat: 4g; Cholesterol: 130mg; Sodium: 1350mg; Total Carbs: 9g; Dietary Fiber: 1g; Total Sugars: 4g; Protein: 35g

Fennel & Chicken Ratatouille

Servings: 4 | Prep Time: 20 Minutes | Cooking Time: 30 Minutes

Ingredients:

- 450g boneless, skinless chicken thighs, cubed
- 2 tbsp grated Parmesan cheese
- 1 eggplant, cubed
- 1 zucchini, cubed
- 1 bell pepper, diced
- 1 fennel bulb, sliced
- 1 tsp salt
- 1 tsp Italian seasoning
- 2 tbsp olive oil
- 1 can (400g) diced tomatoes
- 1 tsp pasta sauce
- 2 tbsp basil leaves

Directions:

1. Preheat air fryer to 200°C/400°F.
2. Mix the chicken, eggplant, zucchini, bell pepper, fennel, salt, Italian seasoning, and oil in a bowl.
3. Place the chicken mixture in the frying basket and Air Fry for 7 minutes. Transfer it to a cake pan.
4. Mix in tomatoes along with juices and pasta sauce. Air Fry for 8 minutes.
5. Scatter with Parmesan and basil. Serve.

Variations & Ingredients Tips:

- ▶ Use other vegetables like mushrooms, onions or summer squash.

- ▶ Substitute fennel with celery for a milder flavor.
- ▶ Serve over pasta, rice or with crusty bread.

Per serving: Calories: 320; Total Fat: 17g; Saturated Fat: 4g; Cholesterol: 105mg; Sodium: 820mg; Total Carbs: 16g; Dietary Fiber: 5g; Total Sugars: 8g; Protein: 27g

Asian Sweet Chili Chicken

Servings: 4 | Prep Time: 15 Minutes | Cooking Time: 30 Minutes

Ingredients:

- 2 chicken breasts, cut into 2.5cm pieces
- 1 cup cornstarch
- 1 tsp chicken seasoning
- Salt and pepper to taste
- 2 eggs
- 1 1/2 cups sweet chili sauce

Directions:

1. Preheat air fryer to 180°C/360°F.
2. Mix cornstarch, chicken seasoning, salt and pepper in a large bowl. In another bowl, beat the eggs.
3. Dip the chicken in the cornstarch mixture to coat. Next, dip the chicken into the egg, then return to the cornstarch.
4. Transfer chicken to the air fryer.
5. Lightly spray all of the chicken with cooking oil.
6. Air Fry for 15-16 minutes, shaking the basket once or until golden.
7. Transfer chicken to a serving dish and drizzle with sweet-and-sour sauce. Serve immediately.

Variations & Ingredients Tips:

- ▶ Use chicken tenders or boneless, skinless thighs instead of breasts.
- ▶ Add 1-2 tsp of sesame oil or soy sauce to the cornstarch coating.
- ▶ Toss with steamed broccoli or stir-fried veggies.

Per serving: Calories: 610; Total Fat: 18g; Saturated Fat: 2g; Cholesterol: 165mg; Sodium: 1020mg; Total Carbs: 82g; Dietary Fiber: 1g; Total Sugars: 30g; Protein: 28g

Chicken Meatballs With A Surprise

Servings: 4 | Prep Time: 15 Minutes | Cooking Time: 35 Minutes

Ingredients:

- 1/3 cup cottage cheese crumbles
- 450g ground chicken
- 1/2 tsp onion powder
- 1/4 cup chopped basil
- 1/2 cup bread crumbs
- 1/2 tsp garlic powder

Directions:

1. Preheat air fryer to 175°C/350°F.
2. Combine the ground chicken, onion powder, basil, cottage cheese, bread crumbs, and garlic powder in a bowl.
3. Form into 18 meatballs, about 2 tbsp each.
4. Place the chicken meatballs in the greased frying basket and Air Fry for 12 minutes, shaking once.
5. Serve.

Variations & Ingredients Tips:

▶ Use ground turkey instead of chicken.
▶ Add grated parmesan or shredded mozzarella cheese.
▶ Serve meatballs with marinara sauce for dipping.

Per Serving (4-5 meatballs): Calories: 230; Total Fat: 8g; Saturated Fat: 2g; Cholesterol: 106mg; Sodium: 384mg; Total Carbs: 14g; Dietary Fiber: 1g; Total Sugars: 1g; Protein: 25g

Chicken Parmesan

Servings: 4 | Prep Time: 15 Minutes | Cooking Time: 11 Minutes

Ingredients:

- 4 chicken tenders
- Italian seasoning
- Salt
- 1/4 cup cornstarch
- 1/2 cup Italian salad dressing
- 1/4 cup panko breadcrumbs
- 1/4 cup grated Parmesan cheese, plus more for serving
- Oil for misting or cooking spray
- 225-g spaghetti, cooked
- 1 (680-g) jar marinara sauce

Directions:

1. Pound chicken tenders until about 3-cm thick.
2. Sprinkle both sides with Italian seasoning and salt.
3. Place cornstarch and salad dressing in separate shallow dishes.
4. In a third dish, mix panko crumbs and Parmesan.
5. Dip chicken in cornstarch, then dressing, then crumb mixture pressing to adhere.
6. Spray chicken with oil on both sides and place in air fryer basket in a single layer.
7. Cook at 200°C/390°F for 5 mins. Spray with more oil, turn chicken and cook 6 more mins until cooked through.
8. Toss cooked spaghetti with marinara sauce.
9. Serve chicken over spaghetti, passing extra Parmesan.

Variations & Ingredients Tips:

▶ Use chicken breast instead of tenders, pounding thin.
▶ Add garlic powder or Italian herbs to the breadcrumb mixture.
▶ Top chicken with mozzarella slices before the last few minutes of cooking.

Per Serving: Calories: 464; Total Fat: 14g; Saturated Fat: 3g; Cholesterol: 50mg; Sodium: 1141mg; Total Carbs: 57g; Dietary Fiber: 4g; Total Sugars: 9g; Protein: 27g

Chicken Cordon Bleu Patties

Servings: 4 | Prep Time: 15 Minutes | Cooking Time: 30 Minutes

Ingredients:

- 1/3 cup grated Fontina cheese
- 3 tbsp milk
- 1/3 cup bread crumbs
- 1 egg, beaten
- 1/2 tsp dried parsley
- Salt and pepper to taste
- 565g ground chicken
- 1/4 cup finely chopped ham

Directions:

1. Preheat air fryer to 175°C/350°F.
2. Mix milk, breadcrumbs, egg, parsley, salt and pepper in a bowl.
3. Using hands, add chicken and gently mix until just combined.
4. Divide into 8 portions and shape into thin patties on waxed paper.
5. On 4 patties, top with ham and Fontina cheese, then place another patty on top.
6. Pinch edges together to seal in filling.
7. Arrange patties in greased air fryer basket and cook for 14-16 minutes until cooked through.
8. Serve and enjoy!

Variations & Ingredients Tips:

▶ Use different cheese like swiss or cheddar.
▶ Add mushrooms or spinach to the filling.
▶ Serve with a mustard or garlic aioli sauce for dipping.

Per Serving: Calories: 368; Total Fat: 14g; Saturated Fat: 5g; Cholesterol: 197mg; Sodium:

536mg; Total Carbs: 17g; Dietary Fiber: 1g; Total Sugars: 1g; Protein: 43g

Crispy Duck With Cherry Sauce

Servings: 2 | Prep Time: 20 Minutes | Cooking Time: 33 Minutes

Ingredients:

- 1 whole duck (up to 2.3 kg), split in half, back and rib bones removed
- 1 teaspoon olive oil
- salt and freshly ground black pepper
- Cherry Sauce:
- 1 tablespoon butter
- 1 shallot, minced
- ½ cup sherry
- ¾ cup cherry preserves
- 1 cup chicken stock
- 1 teaspoon white wine vinegar
- 1 teaspoon fresh thyme leaves
- salt and freshly ground black pepper

Directions:

1. Preheat the air fryer to 200°C/400°F.
2. Trim some of the fat from the duck. Rub olive oil on the duck and season with salt and pepper. Place the duck halves in the air fryer basket, breast side up and facing the center of the basket.
3. Air-fry the duck for 20 minutes. Turn the duck over and air-fry for another 6 minutes.
4. While duck is air-frying, make the cherry sauce. Melt the butter in a large sauté pan. Add the shallot and sauté until it is just starting to brown – about 2 to 3 minutes. Add the sherry and deglaze the pan by scraping up any brown bits from the bottom of the pan. Simmer the liquid for a few minutes, until it has reduced by half. Add the cherry preserves, chicken stock and white wine vinegar. Whisk well to combine all the ingredients. Simmer the sauce until it thickens and coats the back of a spoon – about 5 to 7 minutes. Season with salt and pepper and stir in the fresh thyme leaves.
5. When the air fryer timer goes off, spoon some cherry sauce over the duck and continue to air-fry at 200°C/400°F for 4 more minutes. Then, turn the duck halves back over so that the breast side is facing up. Spoon more cherry sauce over the top of the duck, covering the skin completely. Air-fry for 3 more minutes and then remove the duck to a plate to rest for a few minutes.
6. Serve the duck in halves, or cut each piece in half again for a smaller serving. Spoon any additional sauce over the duck or serve it on the side.

Variations & Ingredients Tips:

▶ Use duck breasts or legs instead of a whole duck for quicker cooking time.

▶ Substitute cherry preserves with blackberry, raspberry, or apricot jam.

▶ Garnish with fresh herbs like rosemary, sage, or parsley before serving.

Per Serving: Calories: 610; Total Fat: 36g; Saturated Fat: 12g; Sodium: 430mg; Total Carbohydrates: 41g; Dietary Fiber: 1g; Total Sugars: 34g; Protein: 34g

Tortilla Crusted Chicken Breast

Servings: 2 | Prep Time: 10 Minutes | Cooking Time: 12 Minutes

Ingredients:

- 1/3 cup flour
- 1 teaspoon salt
- 1 1/2 teaspoons chili powder
- 1 teaspoon ground cumin
- Freshly ground black pepper
- 1 egg, beaten
- 3/4 cup coarsely crushed yellow corn tortilla chips
- 2 (85-115g) boneless chicken breasts
- Vegetable oil
- 1/2 cup salsa
- 1/2 cup crumbled queso fresco
- Fresh cilantro leaves
- Sour cream or guacamole (optional)

Directions:

1. Set up 3 dishes: one with flour+salt+chili powder+cumin+pepper, one with beaten egg, one with crushed tortilla chips.
2. Dredge chicken in flour, then egg, then tortilla chips, pressing to adhere.
3. Spray chicken with oil on both sides.
4. Preheat air fryer to 195°C/380°F.
5. Air fry chicken for 6 mins, flip and cook 6 more mins.
6. Serve with salsa, queso fresco, cilantro, and sour cream/guacamole if desired.

Variations & Ingredients Tips:

▶ Use panko breadcrumbs instead of tortilla chips.

▶ Add lime zest or jalapeño to the breading.

▶ Serve with Mexican rice and beans on the side.

Per Serving: Calories: 471; Total Fat: 19g; Saturated Fat: 4g; Cholesterol: 200mg; Sodium: 1205mg; Total Carbs: 37g; Dietary Fiber: 3g; Total Sugars: 2g; Protein: 36g

Air-fried Turkey Breast With

Cherry Glaze

Servings: 6 | Prep Time: 15 Minutes | Cooking Time: 54 Minutes

Ingredients:

- 1 (2.3kg) turkey breast
- 2 teaspoons olive oil
- 1 teaspoon dried thyme
- 1/2 teaspoon dried sage
- 1 teaspoon salt
- 1/2 teaspoon freshly ground black pepper
- 1/2 cup cherry preserves
- 1 tablespoon chopped fresh thyme leaves
- 1 teaspoon soy sauce
- Freshly ground black pepper

Directions:

1. All turkeys are built differently, so depending on the turkey breast and how your butcher has prepared it, you may need to trim the bottom of the ribs in order to get the turkey to sit upright in the air fryer basket without touching the heating element. The key to this recipe is getting the right size turkey breast. Once you've managed that, the rest is easy, so make sure your turkey breast fits into the air fryer basket before you Preheat the air fryer.
2. Preheat the air fryer to 175°C/350°F.
3. Brush the turkey breast all over with the olive oil. Combine the thyme, sage, salt and pepper and rub the outside of the turkey breast with the spice mixture.
4. Transfer the seasoned turkey breast to the air fryer basket, breast side up, and air-fry at 175°C/350°F for 25 minutes. Turn the turkey breast on its side and air-fry for another 12 minutes. Turn the turkey breast on the opposite side and air-fry for 12 more minutes. The internal temperature of the turkey breast should reach 75°C/165°F when fully cooked.
5. While the turkey is air-frying, make the glaze by combining the cherry preserves, fresh thyme, soy sauce and pepper in a small bowl. When the cooking time is up, return the turkey breast to an upright position and brush the glaze all over the turkey. Air-fry for a final 5 minutes, until the skin is nicely browned and crispy. Let the turkey rest, loosely tented with foil, for at least 5 minutes before slicing and serving.

Variations & Ingredients Tips:

- Use other fruit preserves like orange or cranberry for the glaze.
- Stuff the cavity with aromatics like onion, apple, herbs for extra flavor.
- Brine the turkey breast for 12-24 hours before cooking for juicier meat.

Per serving: Calories: 470; Total Fat: 12g; Saturated Fat: 3g; Cholesterol: 190mg; Sodium: 760mg; Total Carbs: 22g; Dietary Fiber: 0g; Total Sugars: 18g; Protein: 66g

Windsor's Chicken Salad

Servings: 4 | Prep Time: 15 Minutes (plus Chilling Time) | Cooking Time: 30 Minutes

Ingredients:

- 1/2 cup halved seedless red grapes
- 2 chicken breasts, cubed
- Salt and pepper to taste
- 3/4 cup mayonnaise
- 1 tbsp lemon juice
- 2 tbsp chopped parsley
- 1/2 cup chopped celery
- 1 shallot, diced

Directions:

1. Preheat air fryer to 175°C/350°F.
2. Sprinkle chicken with salt and pepper. Place the chicken cubes in the frying basket and Air Fry for 9 minutes, flipping once.
3. In a salad bowl, combine the cooked chicken, mayonnaise, lemon juice, parsley, grapes, celery, and shallot and let chill covered in the fridge for 1 hour up to overnight.

Variations & Ingredients Tips:

- Add chopped toasted pecans or walnuts for crunch.
- Mix in some curry powder or Dijon mustard to the dressing.
- Serve in lettuce cups, sandwiches or wraps.

Per serving: Calories: 470; Total Fat: 40g; Saturated Fat: 7g; Cholesterol: 95mg; Sodium: 380mg; Total Carbs: 6g; Dietary Fiber: 1g; Total Sugars: 4g; Protein: 24g

Gingery Turkey Meatballs

Servings: 4 | Prep Time: 10 Minutes | Cooking Time: 25 Minutes

Ingredients:

- 1/4 cup water chestnuts, chopped
- 1/4 cup panko bread crumbs
- 450g ground turkey
- 1/2 tsp ground ginger
- 2 tbsp fish sauce
- 1 tbsp sesame oil
- 1 small onion, minced
- 1 egg, beaten

Directions:

1. Preheat air fryer to 200°C/400°F.
2. Place the ground turkey, water chestnuts, ground ginger, fish sauce, onion, egg, and bread crumbs in a bowl and stir to combine.
3. Form the turkey mixture into 2.5-cm meatballs. Arrange the meatballs in the baking pan. Drizzle with sesame oil.
4. Bake until the meatballs are cooked through, 10-12 minutes, flipping once.
5. Serve and enjoy!

Variations & Ingredients Tips:

- Add finely grated carrot or zucchini for extra veggies.
- Use soy sauce instead of fish sauce for a milder flavor.
- Serve with sweet chili sauce or teriyaki glaze for dipping.

Per serving: Calories: 320; Total Fat: 21g; Saturated Fat: 5g; Cholesterol: 145mg; Sodium: 820mg; Total Carbs: 6g; Dietary Fiber: 1g; Total Sugars: 1g; Protein: 28g

Pecan Turkey Cutlets

Servings: 4 | Prep Time: 15 Minutes | Cooking Time: 12 Minutes

Ingredients:

- 3/4 cup panko breadcrumbs
- 1/4 teaspoon salt
- 1/4 teaspoon pepper
- 1/4 teaspoon dry mustard
- 1/4 teaspoon poultry seasoning
- 1/2 cup pecans
- 1/4 cup cornstarch
- 1 egg, beaten
- 450g turkey cutlets, 1.3-cm thick
- Salt and pepper
- Oil for misting or cooking spray

Directions:

1. Place the panko crumbs, 1/4 teaspoon salt, 1/4 teaspoon pepper, mustard, and poultry seasoning in food processor. Process until crumbs are finely crushed. Add pecans and process in short pulses just until nuts are finely chopped. Go easy so you don't overdo it!
2. Preheat air fryer to 180°C/360°F.
3. Place cornstarch in one shallow dish and beaten egg in another. Transfer coating mixture from food processor into a third shallow dish.
4. Sprinkle turkey cutlets with salt and pepper to taste.
5. Dip cutlets in cornstarch and shake off excess. Then dip in beaten egg and roll in crumbs, pressing to coat well. Spray both sides with oil or cooking spray.
6. Place 2 cutlets in air fryer basket in a single layer and cook for 12 minutes or until juices run clear.
7. Repeat step 6 to cook remaining cutlets.

Variations & Ingredients Tips:

- Use walnuts, almonds or pistachios instead of pecans.
- Add some grated Parmesan to the breading mixture.
- Serve with a honey mustard or cranberry dipping sauce.

Per serving: Calories: 320; Total Fat: 15g; Saturated Fat: 2g; Cholesterol: 100mg; Sodium: 330mg; Total Carbs: 17g; Dietary Fiber: 2g; Total Sugars: 1g; Protein: 31g

Katsu Chicken Thighs

Servings: 4 | Prep Time: 15 Minutes | Cooking Time: 35 Minutes

Ingredients:

- 680g boneless, skinless chicken thighs
- 3 tbsp tamari sauce
- 3 tbsp lemon juice
- 1/2 tsp ground ginger
- Black pepper to taste
- 6 tbsp cornstarch
- 1 cup chicken stock
- 2 tbsp hoisin sauce
- 2 tbsp light brown sugar
- 2 tbsp sesame seeds

Directions:

1. Preheat the air fryer to 200°C/400°F.
2. After cubing the chicken thighs, put them in a cake pan. Add a tbsp of tamari sauce, a tbsp of lemon juice, ginger, and black pepper. Mix and let marinate for 10 minutes.
3. Remove the chicken and coat it in 4 tbsp of cornstarch; set aside.
4. Add the rest of the marinade to the pan and add the stock, hoisin sauce, brown sugar, and the remaining tamari sauce, lemon juice, and cornstarch. Mix well. Put the pan in the frying basket and Air Fry for 5-8 minutes or until bubbling and thick, stirring once. Remove and set aside.
5. Put the chicken in the frying basket and Fry for 15-18 minutes, shaking the basket once.
6. Remove the chicken to the sauce in the pan and return to the fryer to reheat for 2 minutes. Sprinkle with the sesame seeds and serve.

Variations & Ingredients Tips:

- Use pork chops or firm tofu instead of chicken.
- Add some sriracha or chili garlic sauce to the katsu for heat.

▶ Serve with steamed rice and shredded cabbage.

Per serving: Calories: 400; Total Fat: 14g; Saturated Fat: 3.5g; Cholesterol: 170mg; Sodium: 1210mg; Total Carbs: 27g; Dietary Fiber: 1g; Total Sugars: 9g; Protein: 41g

Curried Chicken Legs

Servings: 4 | Prep Time: 10 Minutes (plus Marinating Time) | Cooking Time: 40 Minutes

Ingredients:

- ¾ cup Greek yogurt
- 1 tbsp tomato paste
- 2 tsp curry powder
- ½ tbsp oregano
- 1 tsp salt
- 680 grams chicken legs
- 2 tbsp chopped fresh mint

Directions:

1. Combine yogurt, tomato paste, curry powder, oregano and salt in a bowl. Divide the mixture in half. Cover one half and store it in the fridge. Into the other half, toss in the chicken until coated and marinate covered in the fridge for 30 minutes up to overnight.
2. Preheat air fryer to 190°C/370°F.
3. Shake excess marinade from chicken. Place chicken legs in the greased air fryer basket and Air Fry for 18 minutes, flipping once and brushing with yogurt mixture.
4. Serve topped with mint.

Variations & Ingredients Tips:

▶ Use chicken drumsticks or thighs instead of legs.

▶ Add minced garlic, ginger, or cayenne pepper to the marinade for extra spice.

▶ Serve with basmati rice, naan bread, and cucumber raita on the side.

Per Serving: Calories: 350; Total Fat: 20g; Saturated Fat: 6g; Sodium: 620mg; Total Carbohydrates: 4g; Dietary Fiber: 1g; Total Sugars: 2g; Protein: 36g

Beef, Pork & Lamb Recipes

Steakhouse Burgers With Red Onion Compote

Servings: 4 | Prep Time: 25 Minutes | Cooking Time: 22 Minutes

Ingredients:

- 680 g lean ground beef
- 2 cloves garlic, minced and divided
- 1 teaspoon Worcestershire sauce
- 1 teaspoon sea salt, divided
- ½ teaspoon black pepper
- 1 tablespoon extra-virgin olive oil
- 1 red onion, thinly sliced
- 59 g balsamic vinegar
- 1 teaspoon sugar
- 1 tablespoon tomato paste
- 2 tablespoons mayonnaise
- 2 tablespoons sour cream
- 4 brioche hamburger buns
- 1 cup arugula

Directions:

1. In a large bowl, mix together the ground beef, 1 of the minced garlic cloves, the Worcestershire sauce, ½ teaspoon of the salt, and the black pepper. Form the meat into 2.5 cm-thick patties. Make a dent in the center (this helps the center cook evenly). Let the meat sit for 15 minutes.
2. Meanwhile, in a small saucepan over medium heat, cook the olive oil and red onion for 4 minutes, stirring frequently to avoid burning. Add in the balsamic vinegar, sugar, and tomato paste, and cook for an additional 3 minutes, stirring frequently. Transfer the onion compote to a small bowl.
3. Preheat the air fryer to 175°C/350°F.
4. In another small bowl, mix together the remaining minced garlic, the mayonnaise, and the sour cream. Spread the mayo mixture on the insides of the brioche buns.
5. Cook the hamburgers for 6 minutes, flip the burgers, and cook an additional 2 to 6 minutes. Check the internal temperature to avoid under- or overcooking. Hamburgers should be cooked to at least 71°C/160°F. After cooking, cover with foil and let the meat rest for 5 minutes.
6. Meanwhile, place the buns inside the air fryer and toast them for 3 minutes.
7. To assemble the burgers, place the hamburger on one side of the bun, top with onion compote and 59 g arugula, and then place the other half of the bun on top.

Variations & Ingredients Tips:

▶ Mix some crumbled blue cheese or crispy bacon into the burger patties

▶ Top with sliced avocado, fried egg or sautéed mushrooms

▶ Swap arugula for watercress, baby spinach or butter lettuce

Per Serving: Calories: 588; Total Fat: 35g; Saturated Fat: 11g; Cholesterol: 124mg; Sodium: 945mg; Total Carbs: 32g; Dietary Fiber: 2g; Total Sugars: 10g; Protein: 39g

Wasabi-coated Pork Loin Chops

Servings: 3 | Prep Time: 15 Minutes | Cooking Time: 14 Minutes

Ingredients:

- 1½ cups Wasabi peas
- ¼ cup Plain panko breadcrumbs
- 1 Large egg white
- 2 tablespoons Water
- 3 (142g each) boneless center-cut pork loin chops (about 1.25cm thick)

Directions:

1. Preheat the air fryer to 190°C/375°F.
2. In a food processor, grind wasabi peas until finely ground like panko crumbs. Add breadcrumbs and pulse to blend.
3. Whisk egg white and water in one shallow dish. Place wasabi pea mixture in another shallow dish.
4. Dip pork chops in egg mixture, allowing excess to drip off, then coat in wasabi mixture, pressing gently.
5. Air fry chops for 12 minutes, flipping halfway, until crisp, browned and internal temp reaches 63°C/145°F (may need 2 extra minutes at 182°C/360°F).
6. Transfer chops to a wire rack and let cool briefly before serving.

Variations & Ingredients Tips:

▶ For extra crunch, double dip the pork chops in the egg and coating mixtures

▶ Add 1-2 tsp wasabi powder to the coating for more heat

▶ Substitute panko with regular breadcrumbs if desired

Per Serving: Calories: 310; Total Fat: 12g; Saturated Fat: 3g; Cholesterol: 105mg; Sodium: 520mg; Total Carbs: 18g; Dietary Fiber: 2g; Total Sugars: 2g; Protein: 33g

Broccoli & Mushroom Beef

Servings: 4 | Prep Time: 10 Minutes | Cooking Time: 30 Minutes

Ingredients:

- 454g sirloin strip steak, cubed
- 227g sliced cremini mushrooms
- 2 tbsp potato starch
- 120ml beef broth
- 5ml soy sauce
- 625g broccoli florets
- 1 onion, chopped
- 1 tbsp grated fresh ginger
- 240g cooked quinoa

Directions:

1. Add potato starch, broth, and soy sauce to a bowl and mix, then add in the beef and coat thoroughly. Marinate for 5 minutes. Preheat air fryer to 400°F/205°C. Set aside the broth and move the beef to a bowl. Add broccoli, onion, mushrooms, and ginger and transfer the bowl to the air fryer. Bake for 12-15 minutes until the beef is golden brown and the veggies soft. Pour the reserved broth over the beef and cook for 2-3 more minutes until the sauce is bubbling. Serve warm over cooked quinoa.

Variations & Ingredients Tips:

▶ Use flank steak or beef tenderloin instead of sirloin

▶ Add bell peppers or snap peas for extra veggies

▶ Thicken the sauce with a cornstarch slurry if desired

Per Serving: Calories 320; Total Fat 10g; Saturated Fat 3g; Cholesterol 60mg; Sodium 380mg; Total Carbs 31g; Fiber 5g; Sugars 4g; Protein 30g

Basil Cheese & Ham Stromboli

Servings: 6 | Prep Time: 15 Minutes | Cooking Time: 30 Minutes

Ingredients:

- 1 can refrigerated pizza dough
- ½ cup shredded mozzarella
- ½ red bell pepper, sliced
- 2 tsp all-purpose flour
- 6 Havarti cheese slices
- 12 deli ham slices
- ½ tsp dried basil
- 1 tsp garlic powder
- ½ tsp oregano
- Black pepper to taste

Directions:

1. Preheat air fryer to 200°C/400°F. Flour a flat work surface and roll out the pizza dough. Use a knife to cut into 6 equal-sized rectangles. On each rectangle, add 1 slice of Havarti, 1 tbsp of mozzarella, 2 slices of ham, and

some red pepper slices. Season with basil, garlic, oregano, and black pepper. Fold one side of the dough over the filling to the opposite side. Press the edges with the back of a fork to seal them. Place one batch of stromboli in the fryer and lightly spray with cooking oil. Air fry for 10 minutes. Serve and enjoy!

Variations & Ingredients Tips:

- Use different cheeses like provolone, Swiss, or cheddar for varied flavors.
- Add sliced olives, mushrooms, or spinach to the filling for extra veggies.
- Serve with marinara sauce or ranch dressing for dipping.

Per Serving: Calories: 303; Total Fat: 15g; Saturated Fat: 8g; Cholesterol: 45mg; Sodium: 793mg; Total Carbohydrates: 27g; Dietary Fiber: 1g; Total Sugars: 4g; Protein: 16g

Sloppy Joes

Servings: 4 | Prep Time: 10 Minutes | Cooking Time: 17 Minutes

Ingredients:

- oil for misting or cooking spray
- 454 g very lean ground beef
- 1 teaspoon onion powder
- ⅓ cup ketchup
- ¼ cup water
- ½ teaspoon celery seed
- 1 tablespoon lemon juice
- 1½ teaspoons brown sugar
- 1¼ teaspoons low-sodium Worcestershire sauce
- ½ teaspoon salt (optional)
- ½ teaspoon vinegar
- ⅛ teaspoon dry mustard
- hamburger or slider buns

Directions:

1. Spray air fryer basket with nonstick cooking spray or olive oil.
2. Break raw ground beef into small chunks and pile into basket.
3. Cook at 195°C/390°F for 5 minutes. Stir to break apart and cook 3 minutes. Stir and cook 4 minutes longer or until meat is well done.
4. Remove meat from air fryer, drain, and use a knife and fork to crumble into small pieces.
5. Give your air fryer basket a quick rinse to remove any bits of meat.
6. Place all the remaining ingredients except the buns in a 15 x 15 cm baking pan and mix together.
7. Add meat and stir well.
8. Cook at 165°C/330°F for 5 minutes. Stir and cook for 2 minutes.
9. Scoop onto buns.

Variations & Ingredients Tips:

- Use ground turkey or chicken for a lighter version
- Add diced bell peppers, carrots or zucchini to the meat mixture for extra veggies
- Top with sliced cheese, pickles or coleslaw for crunch and flavor

Per Serving: Calories: 325; Total Fat: 15g; Saturated Fat: 5g; Cholesterol: 81mg; Sodium: 632mg; Total Carbs: 19g; Dietary Fiber: 1g; Total Sugars: 9g; Protein: 28g

Honey Mustard Pork Roast

Servings: 4 | Prep Time: 10 Minutes | Cooking Time: 50 Minutes

Ingredients:

- 1 boneless pork loin roast
- 2 tbsp Dijon mustard
- 2 tsp olive oil
- 1 tsp honey
- 1 garlic clove, minced
- Salt and pepper to taste
- 1 tsp dried rosemary

Directions:

1. Preheat air fryer to 175°C/350°F. Whisk all ingredients in a bowl. Massage into loin on all sides. Place the loin in the frying basket and Roast for 40 minutes, turning once. Let sit onto a cutting board for 5 minutes before slicing. Serve.

Variations & Ingredients Tips:

- Use whole grain or spicy brown mustard for a bolder flavor
- Add some smoked paprika or cumin to the rub for a smoky twist
- Slice and serve over a salad or in sandwiches for leftovers

Per Serving: Calories: 257; Total Fat: 11g; Saturated Fat: 3g; Cholesterol: 90mg; Sodium: 269mg; Total Carbs: 4g; Dietary Fiber: 0g; Total Sugars: 3g; Protein: 36g

Original Köttbullar

Servings: 4 | Prep Time: 15 Minutes | Cooking Time: 30 Minutes

Ingredients:

- 450 g ground beef
- 1 small onion, chopped
- 1 clove garlic, minced
- ⅓ cup bread crumbs
- 1 egg, beaten
- Salt and pepper to taste
- 1 cup beef broth
- ⅓ cup heavy cream
- 2 tablespoons flour

Directions:

1. Preheat air fryer to 190°C/370°F. Combine beef, onion, garlic, crumbs, egg, salt and pepper in a bowl. Scoop 2 tablespoons of mixture and form meatballs with hands.
2. Place the meatballs in the greased frying basket. Bake for 14 minutes.
3. Meanwhile, stir-fry beef broth and heavy cream in a saucepan over medium heat for 2 minutes; stir in flour. Cover and simmer for 4 minutes or until the sauce thicken.
4. Transfer meatballs to a serving dish and drizzle with sauce. Serve and enjoy!

Variations & Ingredients Tips:

▶ Use different types of ground meat, such as pork or turkey, for a variety of flavors.

▶ Add some grated nutmeg or cardamom to the meatball mixture for a traditional Swedish flavor.

▶ Serve the meatballs with a side of mashed potatoes or lingonberry jam for an authentic Swedish meal.

Per Serving: Calories: 420; Total Fat: 29g; Saturated Fat: 13g; Cholesterol: 155mg; Sodium: 570mg; Total Carbs: 12g; Fiber: 1g; Sugars: 2g; Protein: 29g

Tandoori Lamb Samosas

Servings: 2 | Prep Time: 15 Minutes | Cooking Time: 20 Minutes

Ingredients:

- 170 g ground lamb, sautéed
- 59 g spinach, torn
- ½ onion, minced
- 1 teaspoon tandoori masala
- ½ teaspoon ginger-garlic paste
- ½ teaspoon red chili powder
- ½ teaspoon turmeric powder
- Salt and pepper to taste
- 3 puff dough sheets

Directions:

1. Preheat air fryer to 175°C/350°F. Put the ground lamb, tandoori masala, ginger garlic paste, red chili powder, turmeric powder, salt, and pepper in a bowl and stir to combine. Add in the spinach and onion and stir until the ingredients are evenly blended. Divide the mixture into three equal segments.
2. Lay the pastry dough sheets out on a lightly floured surface. Fill each sheet of dough with one of the three portions of lamb mix, then fold the pastry over into a triangle, sealing the edges with a bit of water. Transfer the samosas to the greased frying basket and Air Fry for 12 minutes, flipping once until the samosas are crispy and flaky. Remove and leave to cool for 5 minutes. Serve.

Variations & Ingredients Tips:

▶ Use ground beef, chicken or potatoes instead of lamb

▶ Add some peas, carrots or cauliflower to the filling

▶ Serve with mint chutney or tamarind sauce for dipping

Per Serving: Calories: 548; Total Fat: 39g; Saturated Fat: 15g; Cholesterol: 86mg; Sodium: 383mg; Total Carbs: 28g; Dietary Fiber: 2g; Total Sugars: 1g; Protein: 25g

Country-style Pork Ribs(2)

Servings: 4 | Prep Time: 10 Minutes | Cooking Time: 50 Minutes

Ingredients:

- 1 teaspoon smoked paprika
- 1 teaspoon ground cumin
- 1 teaspoon garlic powder
- 1 teaspoon onion powder
- 1 tablespoon honey
- ½ teaspoon ground mustard
- Salt and pepper to taste
- 2 tablespoons olive oil
- 1 tablespoon fresh orange juice
- 900 g country-style pork ribs

Directions:

1. Preheat air fryer to 180°C/350°F.
2. Combine all spices and honey in a bowl. In another bowl, whisk olive oil and orange juice and massage onto pork ribs. Sprinkle with the spice mixture.
3. Place the pork ribs in the frying basket and Air Fry for 40 minutes, flipping every 10 minutes.
4. Serve.

Variations & Ingredients Tips:

▶ Use different types of citrus juice, such as lemon or lime, for a variety of flavors.

▶ Add some minced garlic or ginger to the marinade for extra flavor.

▶ Serve the pork ribs with a side of roasted sweet potatoes or grilled corn on the cob for a summer meal.

Per Serving: Calories: 590; Total Fat: 41g; Saturated Fat: 13g; Cholesterol: 165mg; Sodium: 180mg; Total Carbs: 7g; Fiber: 1g; Sugars: 5g; Protein: 47g

Aromatic Pork Tenderloin

Servings: 6 | Prep Time: 10 Minutes | Cooking Time: 65 Minutes

Ingredients:

- 1 pork tenderloin
- 2 tablespoons olive oil
- 2 garlic cloves, minced
- 1 teaspoon dried sage
- 1 teaspoon dried marjoram
- 1 teaspoon dried thyme
- 1 teaspoon paprika
- Salt and pepper to taste

Directions:

1. Preheat air fryer to 180°C/360°F.
2. Drizzle oil over the tenderloin, then rub garlic, sage, marjoram, thyme, paprika, salt and pepper all over.
3. Place the tenderloin in the greased frying basket and Bake for 45 minutes.
4. Flip the pork and cook for another 15 minutes. Check the temperature for doneness.
5. Let the cooked tenderloin rest for 10 minutes before slicing.
6. Serve and enjoy!

Variations & Ingredients Tips:

- Use different herbs and spices, such as rosemary, oregano, or cumin, for a variety of flavors.
- Marinate the pork tenderloin in a mixture of olive oil, lemon juice, garlic, and herbs for extra flavor and tenderness.
- Serve the pork tenderloin with a side of roasted vegetables or mashed potatoes for a complete meal.

Per Serving: Calories: 190; Total Fat: 9g; Saturated Fat: 2g; Cholesterol: 75mg; Sodium: 85mg; Total Carbs: 1g; Fiber: 0g; Sugars: 0g; Protein: 25g

Beef Fajitas

Servings: 2 | Prep Time: 5 Minutes | Cooking Time: 15 Minutes

Ingredients:

- 225 g sliced mushrooms
- ½ onion, cut into half-moons
- 1 tbsp olive oil
- Salt and pepper to taste
- 1 strip steak
- ½ tsp smoked paprika
- ½ tsp fajita seasoning
- 2 tbsp corn

Directions:

1. Preheat air fryer to 200°C/400°F. Combine the olive oil, onion, and salt in a bowl. Add the mushrooms and toss to coat. Spread in the frying basket. Sprinkle steak with salt, paprika, fajita seasoning and black pepper. Place steak on top of the mushroom mixture and air fry for 9 minutes, flipping steak once. Let rest onto a cutting board for 5 minutes before cutting in half. Divide steak, mushrooms, corn, and onions between 2 plates and serve.

Variations & Ingredients Tips:

- Add sliced bell peppers, jalapeños, or zucchini to the vegetable mixture for extra color and crunch.
- Use chicken, shrimp, or tofu instead of steak for different protein options.
- Serve with warm tortillas, rice, or beans for a complete fajita meal.

Per Serving: Calories: 331; Total Fat: 20g; Saturated Fat: 6g; Cholesterol: 74mg; Sodium: 172mg; Total Carbohydrates: 12g; Dietary Fiber: 2g; Total Sugars: 4g; Protein: 28g

Crispy Smoked Pork Chops

Servings: 3 | Prep Time: 10 Minutes | Cooking Time: 8 Minutes

Ingredients:

- ⅔ cup all-purpose flour or tapioca flour
- 1 large egg white(s)
- 2 tablespoons water
- 1½ cups corn flake crumbs (gluten-free, if a concern)
- 3 smoked pork chops (225 g each), 1.25 cm thick, bone-in

Directions:

1. Preheat the air fryer to 190°C/375°F.
2. Set up and fill three shallow soup plates or small pie plates on your counter: one for the flour; one for the egg white(s), whisked with the water until foamy; and one for the corn flake crumbs.
3. Set a chop in the flour and turn it several times, coating both sides and the edges. Gently shake off any excess flour, then set it in the beaten egg white mixture. Turn to coat both sides as well as the edges. Let any excess egg white slip back into the rest, then set the chop in the corn flake crumbs. Turn it several times, pressing

gently to coat the chop evenly on both sides and around the edge. Set the chop aside and continue coating the remaining chop(s) in the same way.

4. Set the chops in the basket with as much air space between them as possible. Air-fry undisturbed for 8 minutes, or until the coating is crunchy and the chops are heated through.
5. Use kitchen tongs to transfer the chops to a wire rack and cool for a couple of minutes before serving.

Variations & Ingredients Tips:

- ▶ Use different types of breading, such as breadcrumbs or crushed potato chips, for a variety of textures.
- ▶ Add some smoked paprika or chili powder to the flour mixture for a smoky and spicy flavor.
- ▶ Serve the pork chops with a side of applesauce or coleslaw for a classic pairing.

Per Serving: Calories: 420; Total Fat: 16g; Saturated Fat: 4g; Cholesterol: 90mg; Sodium: 950mg; Total Carbs: 38g; Fiber: 1g; Sugars: 2g; Protein: 33g

French-style Pork Medallions

Servings: 4 | Prep Time: 10 Minutes | Cooking Time: 25 Minutes

Ingredients:

- 454 g pork medallions
- Salt and pepper to taste
- ½ tsp dried marjoram
- 2 tbsp butter
- 1 tbsp olive oil
- 1 tsp garlic powder
- 1 shallot, diced
- 1 cup chicken stock
- 2 tbsp Dijon mustard
- 2 tbsp grainy mustard
- 1/3 cup heavy cream

Directions:

1. Preheat the air fryer to 175°C/350°F. Pound the pork medallions with a rolling pin to about 6 mm thickness. Rub them with salt, pepper, garlic, and marjoram. Place into the greased frying basket and Bake for 7 minutes or until almost done. Remove and wipe the basket clean. Combine the butter, olive oil, shallot, and stock in a baking pan, and set it in the frying basket. Bake for 5 minutes or until the shallot is crispy and tender. Add the mustard and heavy cream and cook for 4 more minutes or until the mix starts to thicken. Then add the pork to the sauce and cook for 5 more minutes, or until the sauce simmers. Remove and serve warm.

Variations & Ingredients Tips:

- ▶ Try using boneless pork chops instead of medallions

- ▶ Add some sliced mushrooms to the sauce for extra umami flavor
- ▶ Serve with mashed potatoes or egg noodles to soak up the delicious sauce

Per Serving: Calories: 483; Total Fat: 36g; Saturated Fat: 16g; Cholesterol: 146mg; Sodium: 706mg; Total Carbs: 5g; Dietary Fiber: 1g; Total Sugars: 2g; Protein: 35g

Pork & Beef Egg Rolls

Servings: 8 | Prep Time: 25 Minutes | Cooking Time: 8 Minutes

Ingredients:

- 115 g very lean ground beef
- 115 g lean ground pork
- 1 tablespoon soy sauce
- 1 teaspoon olive oil
- ½ cup grated carrots
- 2 green onions, chopped
- 2 cups grated Napa cabbage
- ¼ cup chopped water chestnuts
- ¼ teaspoon salt
- ¼ teaspoon garlic powder
- ¼ teaspoon black pepper
- 1 egg
- 1 tablespoon water
- 8 egg roll wraps
- Oil for misting or cooking spray

Directions:

1. In a large skillet, brown beef and pork with soy sauce. Remove cooked meat from skillet, drain, and set aside.
2. Pour off any excess grease from skillet. Add olive oil, carrots, and onions. Sauté until barely tender, about 1 minute.
3. Stir in cabbage, cover, and cook for 1 minute or just until cabbage slightly wilts. Remove from heat.
4. In a large bowl, combine the cooked meats and vegetables, water chestnuts, salt, garlic powder, and pepper. Stir well. If needed, add more salt to taste.
5. Beat together egg and water in a small bowl.
6. Fill egg roll wrappers, using about ¼ cup of filling for each wrap. Roll up and brush all over with egg wash to seal. Spray very lightly with olive oil or cooking spray.
7. Place 4 egg rolls in air fryer basket and cook at 200°C/390°F for 4 minutes. Turn over and cook 4 more minutes, until golden brown and crispy.
8. Repeat to cook remaining egg rolls.

Variations & Ingredients Tips:

- ▶ Use different types of vegetables, such as bean sprouts or bamboo shoots, for a variety of flavors and textures.
- ▶ Add some minced ginger or sesame oil to the filling

for extra flavor.

- ▶ Serve the egg rolls with a side of sweet and sour sauce or hot mustard for dipping.

Per Serving: Calories: 200; Total Fat: 8g; Saturated Fat: 2g; Cholesterol: 50mg; Sodium: 470mg; Total Carbs: 21g; Fiber: 1g; Sugars: 1g; Protein: 11g

Boneless Ribeyes

Servings: 2 | Prep Time: 5 Minutes | Cooking Time: 10-15 Minutes

Ingredients:

- 2 (227g) boneless ribeye steaks
- 4 teaspoons Worcestershire sauce
- 1/2 teaspoon garlic powder
- Pepper
- 4 teaspoons extra virgin olive oil
- Salt

Directions:

1. Season steaks on both sides with Worcestershire sauce. Use the back of a spoon to spread evenly.
2. Sprinkle both sides of steaks with garlic powder and coarsely ground black pepper to taste.
3. Drizzle both sides of steaks with olive oil, again using the back of a spoon to spread evenly over surfaces.
4. Allow steaks to marinate for 30 minutes.
5. Place both steaks in air fryer basket and cook at 198°C/390°F for 5 minutes.
6. Turn steaks over and cook until done: Medium rare: additional 5 minutes Medium: additional 7 minutes Well done: additional 10 minutes
7. Remove steaks from air fryer basket and let sit 5 minutes. Salt to taste and serve.

Variations & Ingredients Tips:

- ▶ Use your preferred steak rub blend instead of just garlic powder and pepper
- ▶ Baste with butter or steak sauce halfway through cooking for extra moisture
- ▶ Let steaks rest 10 minutes before slicing for maximum juiciness

Per Serving: 510 Calories; 38g Total Fat; 15g Saturated Fat; 145mg Cholesterol; 340mg Sodium; 1g Total Carbs; 0g Fiber; 0g Sugars; 43g Protein

Coffee-rubbed Pork Tenderloin

Servings: 4 | Prep Time: 10 Minutes | Cooking Time: 30 Minutes

Ingredients:

- 1 tablespoon packed brown sugar
- 2 teaspoons espresso powder
- 1 teaspoon bell pepper powder
- 1/2 teaspoon dried parsley
- 1 tablespoon honey
- 1/2 tablespoon lemon juice
- 2 teaspoons olive oil
- 450 g pork tenderloin

Directions:

1. Preheat air fryer to 200°C/400°F.
2. Toss the brown sugar, espresso powder, bell pepper powder, and parsley in a bowl and mix together. Add the honey, lemon juice, and olive oil, then stir well.
3. Smear the pork with the mix, then allow to marinate for 10 minutes before putting it in the air fryer.
4. Roast for 9-11 minutes until the pork is cooked through.
5. Slice before serving.

Variations & Ingredients Tips:

- ▶ Use different types of coffee, such as dark roast or decaf, for a variety of flavors.
- ▶ Add some smoked paprika or chili powder to the rub for a spicy kick.
- ▶ Serve the pork tenderloin with a side of roasted vegetables or mashed potatoes for a complete meal.

Per Serving: Calories: 220; Total Fat: 8g; Saturated Fat: 2g; Cholesterol: 75mg; Sodium: 75mg; Total Carbs: 11g; Fiber: 0g; Sugars: 9g; Protein: 27g

Orange Glazed Pork Tenderloin

Servings: 3 | Prep Time: 10 Minutes | Cooking Time: 23 Minutes

Ingredients:

- 2 tablespoons brown sugar
- 2 teaspoons cornstarch
- 2 teaspoons Dijon mustard
- 1/2 cup orange juice
- 1/2 teaspoon soy sauce
- 2 teaspoons grated fresh ginger
- 1/4 cup white wine
- Zest of 1 orange
- 450 g pork tenderloin
- Salt and freshly ground black pepper
- Oranges, halved (for garnish)
- Fresh parsley or other green herb (for garnish)

Directions:

1. Combine the brown sugar, cornstarch, Dijon mustard, orange juice, soy sauce, ginger, white wine and orange zest in a small saucepan and bring the mixture to a boil

43

on the stovetop. Lower the heat and simmer while you cook the pork tenderloin or until the sauce has thickened.
2. Preheat the air fryer to 190°C/370°F.
3. Season all sides of the pork tenderloin with salt and freshly ground black pepper. Transfer the tenderloin to the air fryer basket, bending the pork into a wide "U" shape if necessary to fit in the basket. Air-fry at 190°C/370°F for 20 to 23 minutes, or until the internal temperature reaches 65°C/145°F. Flip the tenderloin over halfway through the cooking process and baste with the sauce.
4. Transfer the tenderloin to a cutting board and let it rest for 5 minutes. Slice the pork at a slight angle and serve immediately with orange halves and fresh herbs to dress it up. Drizzle any remaining glaze over the top.

Variations & Ingredients Tips:

▶ Use different types of citrus, such as lemon or lime, for a variety of flavors.

▶ Add some minced garlic or red pepper flakes to the glaze for extra flavor.

▶ Serve the pork tenderloin with a side of roasted vegetables or rice for a complete meal.

Per Serving: Calories: 310; Total Fat: 6g; Saturated Fat: 2g; Cholesterol: 110mg; Sodium: 370mg; Total Carbs: 22g; Fiber: 1g; Sugars: 17g; Protein: 38g

Apple Cornbread Stuffed Pork Loin With Apple Gravy

Servings: 4 | Prep Time: 20 Minutes | Cooking Time: 61 Minutes

Ingredients:

- 4 strips of bacon, chopped
- 1 Granny Smith apple, peeled, cored and finely chopped
- 2 teaspoons fresh thyme leaves
- ¼ cup chopped fresh parsley
- 2 cups cubed cornbread
- ½ cup chicken stock
- Salt and freshly ground black pepper
- 1 (900 g) boneless pork loin
- Kitchen twine
- Apple Gravy:
- 2 tablespoons butter
- 1 shallot, minced
- 1 Granny Smith apple, peeled, cored and finely chopped
- 3 sprigs fresh thyme
- 2 tablespoons flour
- 1 cup chicken stock
- ½ cup apple cider
- Salt and freshly ground black pepper, to taste

Directions:

1. Preheat the air fryer to 200°C/400°F.
2. Add the bacon to the air fryer and air-fry for 6 minutes until crispy. While the bacon is cooking, combine the apple, fresh thyme, parsley and cornbread in a bowl and toss well. Moisten the mixture with the chicken stock and season to taste with salt and freshly ground black pepper. Add the cooked bacon to the mixture.
3. Butterfly the pork loin by holding it flat on the cutting board with one hand, while slicing into the pork loin parallel to the cutting board with the other. Slice into the longest side of the pork loin, but stop before you cut all the way through. You should then be able to open the pork loin up like a book, making it twice as wide as it was when you started. Season the inside of the pork with salt and freshly ground black pepper.
4. Spread the cornbread mixture onto the butterflied pork loin, leaving a 2.5-cm border around the edge of the pork. Roll the pork loin up around the stuffing to enclose the stuffing, and tie the rolled pork in several places with kitchen twine or secure with toothpicks. Try to replace any stuffing that falls out of the roast as you roll it, by stuffing it into the ends of the rolled pork. Season the outside of the pork with salt and freshly ground black pepper.
5. Preheat the air fryer to 180°C/360°F.
6. Place the stuffed pork loin into the air fryer, seam side down. Air-fry the pork loin for 15 minutes at 180°C/360°F. Turn the pork loin over and air-fry for an additional 15 minutes. Turn the pork loin a quarter turn and air-fry for an additional 15 minutes. Turn the pork loin over again to expose the fourth side, and air-fry for an additional 10 minutes. The pork loin should register 70°C/155°F on an instant read thermometer when it is finished.
7. While the pork is cooking, make the apple gravy. Preheat a saucepan over medium heat on the stovetop and melt the butter. Add the shallot, apple and thyme sprigs and sauté until the apple starts to soften and brown a little. Add the flour and stir for a minute or two. Whisk in the stock and apple cider vigorously to prevent the flour from forming lumps. Bring the mixture to a boil to thicken and season to taste with salt and pepper.
8. Transfer the pork loin to a resting plate and loosely tent with foil, letting the pork rest for at least 5 minutes before slicing and serving with the apple gravy poured over the top.

Variations & Ingredients Tips:

▶ Use different types of bread, such as sourdough or whole wheat, for the stuffing for a variety of flavors and textures.

- ▶ Add some chopped nuts, such as pecans or walnuts, to the stuffing for a crunchy texture.
- ▶ Serve the pork loin with a side of roasted root vegetables or sautéed greens for a complete meal.

Per Serving: Calories: 690; Total Fat: 35g; Saturated Fat: 12g; Cholesterol: 180mg; Sodium: 780mg; Total Carbs: 37g; Fiber: 3g; Sugars: 15g; Protein: 58g

Easy Tex-mex Chimichangas

Servings: 2 | Prep Time: 10 Minutes | Cooking Time: 8 Minutes

Ingredients:

- 115 g thinly sliced deli roast beef, chopped
- ½ cup (about 55 g) shredded Cheddar cheese or shredded Tex-Mex cheese blend
- ¼ cup jarred salsa verde or salsa rojo
- ½ teaspoon ground cumin
- ½ teaspoon dried oregano
- 2 burrito-size (30 cm) flour tortilla(s), not corn tortillas (gluten-free, if a concern)
- ⅔ cup canned refried beans
- Vegetable oil spray

Directions:

1. Preheat the air fryer to 190°C/375°F.
2. Stir the roast beef, cheese, salsa, cumin, and oregano in a bowl until well mixed.
3. Lay a tortilla on a clean, dry work surface. Spread ⅓ cup of the refried beans in the center lower third of the tortilla(s), leaving an 2.5-cm on either side of the spread beans.
4. For one chimichanga, spread all of the roast beef mixture on top of the beans. For two, spread half of the roast beef mixture on each tortilla.
5. At either "end" of the filling mixture, fold the sides of the tortilla up and over the filling, partially covering it. Starting with the unfolded side of the tortilla just below the filling, roll the tortilla closed. Fold and roll the second filled tortilla, as necessary.
6. Coat the exterior of the tortilla(s) with vegetable oil spray. Set the chimichanga(s) seam side down in the basket, with at least 1.25 cm air space between them if you're working with two. Air-fry undisturbed for 8 minutes, or until the tortilla is lightly browned and crisp.
7. Use kitchen tongs to gently transfer the chimichanga(s) to a wire rack. Cool for at last 5 minutes or up to 20 minutes before serving.

Variations & Ingredients Tips:

- ▶ Use different types of meat, such as chicken or pork, for a variety of flavors and textures.
- ▶ Add some diced onion or bell pepper to the filling for extra vegetables.
- ▶ Serve the chimichangas with sour cream, guacamole, or extra salsa for dipping.

Per Serving: Calories: 520; Total Fat: 25g; Saturated Fat: 11g; Cholesterol: 65mg; Sodium: 1400mg; Total Carbs: 45g; Fiber: 6g; Sugars: 3g; Protein: 30g

Extra Crispy Country-style Pork Riblets

Servings: 3 | Prep Time: 10 Minutes | Cooking Time: 30 Minutes

Ingredients:

- ⅓ cup Tapioca flour
- 2½ tbsp Chile powder
- ¾ tsp Table salt (optional)
- 567 g Boneless country-style pork ribs, cut into 3.8 cm chunks
- Vegetable oil spray

Directions:

1. Preheat the air fryer to 190°C/375°F.
2. Mix the tapioca flour, chile powder, and salt (if using) in a large bowl until well combined. Add the country-style rib chunks and toss well to coat thoroughly.
3. When the machine is at temperature, gently shake off any excess tapioca coating from the chunks. Generously coat them on all sides with vegetable oil spray. Arrange the chunks in the basket in one layer. The pieces may touch. Air-fry for 30 minutes, rearranging the pieces at the 10- and 20-minute marks to expose any touching bits, until very crisp and well browned.
4. Gently pour the contents of the basket onto a wire rack. Cool for 5 minutes before serving.

Variations & Ingredients Tips:

- ▶ For a smokier flavor, add some smoked paprika to the tapioca mixture
- ▶ Serve with your favorite BBQ sauce or hot sauce for dipping
- ▶ Make sure to cut the pork into even-sized chunks for even cooking

Per Serving: Calories: 381; Total Fat: 19g; Saturated Fat: 5g; Cholesterol: 133mg; Sodium: 324mg; Total Carbs: 11g; Dietary Fiber: 1g; Total Sugars: 0g; Protein: 41g

Fish And Seafood Recipes

Sesame-crusted Tuna Steaks

Servings: 3 | Prep Time: 10 Minutes | Cooking Time: 10-13 Minutes

Ingredients:

- 1/2 cup sesame seeds, preferably a blend of white and black
- 1 1/2 tablespoons toasted sesame oil
- 3 (170g) skinless tuna steaks

Directions:

1. Preheat air fryer to 200°C/400°F.
2. Pour sesame seeds on a plate. Rub 1/2 tbsp sesame oil on both sides and edges of each tuna steak.
3. Dredge steaks in sesame seeds, pressing gently to adhere seeds all over.
4. Place steaks spaced apart in air fryer basket.
5. Air-fry 10 mins for medium-rare, 12-13 mins for cooked through.
6. Transfer steaks to plates and serve hot.

Variations & Ingredients Tips:

- Add lemon or lime zest to the sesame seed coating.
- Brush steaks with teriyaki sauce before coating.
- Serve over salad greens or stir-fried veggies.

Per serving: Calories: 300; Total Fat: 15g; Saturated Fat: 3g; Cholesterol: 60mg; Sodium: 65mg; Total Carbs: 8g; Dietary Fiber: 2g; Sugars: 1g; Protein: 33g

Easy Scallops With Lemon Butter

Servings: 3 | Prep Time: 5 Minutes | Cooking Time: 4 Minutes

Ingredients:

- 1 tablespoon olive oil
- 2 teaspoons minced garlic
- 1 teaspoon finely grated lemon zest
- 1/2 teaspoon red pepper flakes
- 1/4 teaspoon table salt
- 450g sea scallops
- 3 tablespoons butter, melted
- 1 1/2 tablespoons lemon juice

Directions:

1. Preheat the air fryer to 200°C/400°F.
2. Gently stir the olive oil, garlic, lemon zest, red pepper flakes, and salt in a bowl. Add the scallops and stir very gently until they are evenly and well coated.
3. When the machine is at temperature, arrange the scallops in a single layer in the basket. Some may touch Air-fry undisturbed for 4 minutes, or until the scallops are opaque and firm.
4. While the scallops cook, stir the melted butter and lemon juice in a serving bowl. When the scallops are ready, pour them from the basket into this bowl. Toss well before serving.

Variations & Ingredients Tips:

- Add some capers, diced tomatoes or chopped parsley to the sauce.
- Use lime juice and cilantro instead of lemon and parsley for a Mexican twist.
- Serve over angel hair pasta, risotto or sautéed spinach.

Per serving: Calories: 330; Total Fat: 21g; Saturated Fat: 10g; Cholesterol: 110mg; Sodium: 940mg; Total Carbs: 4g; Dietary Fiber: 0g; Total Sugars: 0g; Protein: 31g

Saucy Shrimp

Servings: 4 | Prep Time: 15 Minutes | Cooking Time: 30 Minutes

Ingredients:

- 450g peeled shrimp, deveined
- 1/2 cup grated coconut
- 1/4 cup bread crumbs
- 1/4 cup flour
- 1/4 tsp smoked paprika
- Salt and pepper to taste
- 1 egg
- 2 tbsp maple syrup
- 1/2 tsp rice vinegar
- 1 tbsp hot sauce
- 1/8 tsp red pepper flakes
- 1/4 cup orange juice
- 1 tsp cornstarch
- 1/2 cup banana ketchup
- 1 lemon, sliced

Directions:

1. Preheat air fryer to 175°C/350°F.
2. Combine coconut, crumbs, flour, paprika, salt & pepper in a bowl.
3. In another bowl, whisk egg with 1 tsp water.
4. Dip shrimp in egg, then coat in crumb mixture.
5. Arrange shrimp in greased frying basket. Air Fry 5 mins, flip and cook 2-3 more mins.

46

6. Make sauce: In a pan, add syrup, ketchup, hot sauce, vinegar, pepper flakes. Make slurry with OJ and cornstarch.
7. Add slurry to pan, boil 5 mins until thick. Let sit 5 mins.
8. Serve shrimp with sauce and lemon wedges.

Variations & Ingredients Tips:

- Substitute honey or agave for maple syrup.
- Add chopped pineapple or mango to the sauce.
- Toss cooked shrimp in the sauce instead of serving on the side.

Per serving: Calories: 290; Total Fat: 7g; Saturated Fat: 4g; Cholesterol: 170mg; Sodium: 1050mg; Total Carbs: 37g; Dietary Fiber: 2g; Sugars: 17g; Protein: 20g

French Grouper Nicoise

Servings: 4 | Prep Time: 10 Minutes | Cooking Time: 20 Minutes

Ingredients:

- 4 grouper fillets
- Salt to taste
- 1/2 tsp ground cumin
- 3 garlic cloves, minced
- 1 tomato, sliced
- 1/4 cup sliced Nicoise olives
- 1/4 cup dill, chopped
- 1 lemon, juiced
- 1/4 cup olive oil

Directions:

1. Preheat air fryer to 195°C/380°F.
2. Season grouper fillets with salt and cumin.
3. Arrange fillets in greased air fryer basket.
4. Top with garlic, tomato, olives and fresh dill.
5. Drizzle with lemon juice and olive oil.
6. Bake for 10-12 minutes.
7. Serve and enjoy!

Variations & Ingredients Tips:

- Use other white fish like halibut or cod.
- Add capers, red onion or roasted red peppers.
- Serve over arugula or with roasted potatoes.

Per Serving: Calories: 275; Total Fat: 13g; Saturated Fat: 2g; Cholesterol: 86mg; Sodium: 267mg; Total Carbs: 3g; Dietary Fiber: 1g; Total Sugars: 0g; Protein: 35g

Feta & Shrimp Pita

Servings: 4 | Prep Time: 10 Minutes | Cooking Time: 15 Minutes

Ingredients:

- 450g peeled shrimp, deveined
- 2 tbsp olive oil
- 1 tsp dried oregano
- 1/2 tsp dried thyme
- 1/2 tsp garlic powder
- 1/4 tsp shallot powder
- 1/4 tsp tarragon powder
- Salt and pepper to taste
- 4 whole-wheat pitas
- 115g feta cheese, crumbled
- 1 cup grated lettuce
- 1 tomato, diced
- 1/4 cup black olives, sliced
- 1 lemon

Directions:

1. Preheat oven to 195°C/380°F.
2. Mix shrimp with oil, oregano, thyme, garlic, shallot, tarragon powders, salt and pepper.
3. Pour shrimp in air fryer basket and bake 6-8 mins until cooked through.
4. Divide shrimp into warmed pitas with feta, lettuce, tomato, olives and lemon squeeze.
5. Serve and enjoy!

Variations & Ingredients Tips:

- Use cooked chicken instead of shrimp.
- Add sliced red onion or cucumber to the pita filling.
- Drizzle with tzatziki sauce instead of lemon juice.

Per Serving: Calories: 331; Total Fat: 14g; Saturated Fat: 4g; Cholesterol: 236mg; Sodium: 704mg; Total Carbs: 29g; Dietary Fiber: 4g; Total Sugars: 3g; Protein: 26g

Buttered Swordfish Steaks

Servings: 4 | Prep Time: 15 Minutes | Cooking Time: 30 Minutes

Ingredients:

- 4 swordfish steaks
- 2 eggs, beaten
- 85 grams melted butter
- ½ cup breadcrumbs
- Black pepper to taste
- 1 tsp dried rosemary
- 1 tsp dried marjoram
- 1 lemon, cut into wedges

Directions:

1. Preheat air fryer to 180°C/350°F.
2. Place the eggs and melted butter in a bowl and stir thoroughly.
3. Combine the breadcrumbs, rosemary, marjoram, and black pepper in a separate bowl.
4. Dip the swordfish steaks in the beaten eggs, then coat

with the crumb mixture.
5. Place the coated fish in the air fryer basket.
6. Air Fry for 12-14 minutes, turning once until the fish is cooked through and the crust is toasted and crispy.
7. Serve with lemon wedges.

Variations & Ingredients Tips:

- Use cod, halibut, or mahi-mahi instead of swordfish for different fish options.
- Add grated Parmesan cheese or finely chopped nuts to the breading for extra flavor and texture.
- Serve with tartar sauce, garlic aioli, or a side of roasted vegetables.

Per Serving: Calories: 420; Total Fat: 27g; Saturated Fat: 15g; Sodium: 330mg; Total Carbohydrates: 11g; Dietary Fiber: 1g; Total Sugars: 1g; Protein: 33g

Kid's Flounder Fingers

Servings: 4 | Prep Time: 10 Minutes | Cooking Time: 45 Minutes

Ingredients:

- 450g catfish flounder fillets, cut into 2.5cm chunks
- 1/2 cup seasoned fish fry breading mix

Directions:

1. Preheat air fryer to 200°C/400°F.
2. In a resealable bag, add flounder chunks and breading mix.
3. Seal and shake bag until fish is coated.
4. Place coated nuggets in a single layer in greased air fryer basket.
5. Air fry for 18-20 minutes, shaking basket once, until crisp.
6. Serve warm.

Variations & Ingredients Tips:

- Use any firm white fish like cod or haddock.
- Make your own seasoned breadcrumb mix with spices.
- Serve with tartar sauce, ketchup or ranch for dipping.

Per Serving: Calories: 167; Total Fat: 2g; Saturated Fat: 0g; Cholesterol: 51mg; Sodium: 513mg; Total Carbs: 13g; Dietary Fiber: 0g; Total Sugars: 1g; Protein: 23g

Shrimp Po'boy With Remoulade Sauce

Servings: 6 | Prep Time: 10 Minutes | Cooking Time: 8 Minutes

Ingredients:

- 1/2 cup all-purpose flour
- 1/2 teaspoon paprika
- 1 teaspoon garlic powder
- 1/2 teaspoon black pepper
- 1/4 teaspoon salt
- 2 eggs, whisked
- 1 1/2 cups panko breadcrumbs
- 450g small shrimp peeled and deveined
- Six 15-cm French rolls
- 2 cups shredded lettuce
- 12 0.3-cm tomato slices
- 3/4 cup Remoulade Sauce

Directions:

1. Preheat air fryer to 180°C/360°F.
2. Mix flour, paprika, garlic, pepper and salt in a bowl.
3. Place eggs in a dish. Place panko in another dish.
4. Coat shrimp in flour, dip in egg, then coat in panko.
5. Spray air fryer trivet/basket with oil. Add shrimp in a single layer, spacing apart.
6. Cook 4 mins, flip and cook 4 more mins until crispy.
7. Build sandwiches with rolls, lettuce, tomato, shrimp and remoulade sauce.

Variations & Ingredients Tips:

- Use your favorite store-bought or homemade remoulade.
- Add sliced avocado or pickles to the sandwiches.
- Serve shrimp over salad greens instead of on a roll.

Per serving: Calories: 340; Total Fat: 8g; Saturated Fat: 1g; Cholesterol: 215mg; Sodium: 790mg; Total Carbs: 45g; Dietary Fiber: 2g; Sugars: 4g; Protein: 22g

Basil Crab Cakes With Fresh Salad

Servings: 2 | Prep Time: 15 Minutes | Cooking Time: 25 Minutes

Ingredients:

- 225g lump crabmeat
- 2 tbsp mayonnaise
- 1/2 tsp Dijon mustard
- 1/2 tsp lemon juice
- 1/2 tsp lemon zest
- 2 tsp minced yellow onion
- 1/4 tsp prepared horseradish
- 1/4 cup flour

- 1 egg white, beaten
- 1 tbsp basil, minced
- 1 tbsp olive oil
- 2 tsp white wine vinegar
- Salt and pepper to taste
- 115g arugula
- 1/2 cup blackberries
- 1/4 cup pine nuts
- 2 lemon wedges

Directions:

1. Preheat air fryer to 200°C/400°F.
2. Combine the crabmeat, mayonnaise, mustard, lemon juice and zest, onion, horseradish, flour, egg white, and basil in a bowl. Form mixture into 4 patties.
3. Place the patties in the lightly greased frying basket and Air Fry for 10 minutes, flipping once.
4. Combine olive oil, vinegar, salt, and pepper in a bowl. Toss in the arugula and share into 2 medium bowls. Add 2 crab cakes to each bowl and scatter with blackberries, pine nuts, and lemon wedges.
5. Serve warm.

Variations & Ingredients Tips:

- Add some diced red bell pepper or celery to the crab cake mixture.
- Use mixed greens or baby spinach instead of arugula.
- Serve with a remoulade or spicy mayo sauce.

Per serving: Calories: 440; Total Fat: 29g; Saturated Fat: 4g; Cholesterol: 115mg; Sodium: 830mg; Total Carbs: 19g; Dietary Fiber: 4g; Total Sugars: 6g; Protein: 30g

Mahi Mahi With Cilantro-chili Butter

Servings: 4 | Prep Time: 10 Minutes | Cooking Time: 20 Minutes

Ingredients:

- Salt and pepper to taste
- 4 mahi-mahi fillets
- 2 tbsp butter, melted
- 2 garlic cloves, minced
- 1/4 tsp chili powder
- 1/4 tsp lemon zest
- 1 tsp ginger, minced
- 1 tsp Worcestershire sauce
- 1 tbsp lemon juice
- 1 tbsp chopped cilantro

Directions:

1. Preheat air fryer to 190°C/375°F.
2. Combine butter, Worcestershire sauce, garlic, salt, lemon juice, ginger, pepper, lemon zest, and chili powder in a small bowl.
3. Place the mahi-mahi on a large plate, then spread the seasoned butter on the top of each.
4. Arrange the fish in a single layer in the parchment-lined frying basket. Bake for 6 minutes, then carefully flip the fish.
5. Bake for another 6-7 minutes until the fish is flaky and cooked through.
6. Serve immediately sprinkled with cilantro and enjoy.

Variations & Ingredients Tips:

- Use other firm white fish like cod or halibut.
- Add some cayenne pepper for extra heat.
- Serve over rice or with roasted vegetables.

Per serving: Calories: 200; Total Fat: 8g; Saturated Fat: 4g; Cholesterol: 120mg; Sodium: 220mg; Total Carbs: 2g; Dietary Fiber: 0g; Total Sugars: 0g; Protein: 29g

Fish-in-chips

Servings: 4 | Prep Time: 15 Minutes | Cooking Time: 11 Minutes

Ingredients:

- 1 cup all-purpose flour or potato starch
- 2 large eggs, well beaten
- 1 1/2 cups crushed plain potato chips, preferably thick-cut or ruffled (gluten-free, if a concern)
- 4 (115g) skinless cod fillets

Directions:

1. Preheat the air fryer to 200°C/400°F.
2. Set up and fill three shallow soup plates or small pie plates on your counter: one for the flour, one for the beaten eggs, and one for the crushed potato chips.
3. Dip a piece of cod in the flour, turning it to coat on all sides, even the ends and sides. Gently shake off any excess flour, then dip it in the beaten eggs. Gently turn to coat it on all sides, then let any excess egg slip back into the rest. Set the fillet in the crushed potato chips and turn several times and onto all sides, pressing gently to coat the fish. Dip it back in the eggs, coating all sides but taking care that the coating doesn't slip off; then dip it back in the potato chips for a thick, even coating. Set it aside and coat more fillets in the same way.
4. When the machine is at temperature, set the fillets in the basket with as much air space between them as possible. Air-fry undisturbed for 11 minutes, until golden brown and firm but not hard.
5. Use kitchen tongs to transfer the fillets to a wire rack. Cool for just a minute or two before serving.

Variations & Ingredients Tips:

- Use haddock, pollack or halibut instead of cod.
- Season the flour with Old Bay, lemon pepper or Cajun spice mix.
- Serve with tartar sauce, coleslaw and lemon wedges.

Per serving: Calories: 310; Total Fat: 10g; Saturated Fat: 2g; Cholesterol: 125mg; Sodium: 220mg; Total Carbs: 29g; Dietary Fiber: 1g; Total Sugars: 0g; Protein: 26g

Potato-wrapped Salmon Fillets

Servings: 3 | Prep Time: 15 Minutes | Cooking Time: 8 Minutes

Ingredients:
- 1 (450g) Large elongated yellow potato, peeled
- 3 (170g), 4cm-wide, thick skinless salmon fillets
- Olive oil spray
- 1/4 teaspoon Table salt
- 1/4 teaspoon Ground black pepper

Directions:
1. Preheat the air fryer to 200°C/400°F.
2. Use a peeler or mandoline to make long strips from the potato. You'll need 8 to 12 strips per fillet.
3. Drape potato strips over a salmon fillet, overlapping to create an even "crust." Tuck strips under the fillet, overlapping underneath. Wrap remaining fillets the same way.
4. Gently turn over fillets. Generously coat bottoms with olive oil spray. Turn back seam-side down and coat tops with oil spray. Sprinkle with salt and pepper.
5. Transfer fillets seam-side down to air fryer basket, leaving space between them. Air-fry 8 minutes until golden brown and crisp.
6. Transfer fillets to plates. Cool briefly before serving.

Variations & Ingredients Tips:
- Use sweet potatoes instead of regular potatoes.
- Add herbs or spices to the potato crust.
- Serve with lemon wedges and tartar sauce.

Per serving: Calories: 390; Total Fat: 16g; Saturated Fat: 3g; Cholesterol: 100mg; Sodium: 280mg; Total Carbs: 23g; Dietary Fiber: 2g; Sugars: 1g; Protein: 37g

Holiday Lobster Salad

Servings: 2 | Prep Time: 10 Minutes | Cooking Time: 20 Minutes

Ingredients:
- 2 lobster tails
- 1/4 cup mayonnaise
- 2 tsp lemon juice
- 1 stalk celery, sliced
- 2 tsp chopped chives
- 2 tsp chopped tarragon
- Salt and pepper to taste
- 2 tomato slices
- 4 cucumber slices
- 1 avocado, diced

Directions:
1. Preheat air fryer to 200°C/400°F.
2. Using kitchen shears, cut down the middle of each lobster tail on the softer side. Carefully run your finger between the lobster meat and the shell to loosen meat.
3. Place lobster tails, cut sides up, in the frying basket, and Air Fry for 8 minutes. Transfer to a large plate and let cool for 3 minutes until easy to handle, then pull lobster meat from the shell and roughly chop it.
4. Combine chopped lobster, mayonnaise, lemon juice, celery, chives, tarragon, salt, and pepper in a bowl.
5. Divide between 2 medium plates and top with tomato slices, cucumber and avocado cubes.
6. Serve immediately.

Variations & Ingredients Tips:
- Substitute lobster with crab, shrimp or crayfish.
- Add some diced red onion or fennel for crunch.
- Serve in lettuce cups, avocado halves or toasted rolls.

Per serving: Calories: 440; Total Fat: 35g; Saturated Fat: 5g; Cholesterol: 130mg; Sodium: 620mg; Total Carbs: 12g; Dietary Fiber: 6g; Total Sugars: 3g; Protein: 24g

Fish Tortillas With Coleslaw

Servings: 4 | Prep Time: 15 Minutes | Cooking Time: 30 Minutes

Ingredients:
- 1 tbsp olive oil
- 450g cod fillets
- 3 tbsp lemon juice
- 2 cups chopped red cabbage
- 1/2 cup salsa
- 1/3 cup sour cream
- 6 taco shells, warm
- 1 avocado, chopped

Directions:
1. Preheat air fryer to 200°C/400°F.
2. Brush oil on the cod and sprinkle with some lemon juice. Place in the frying basket and Air Fry until the fish flakes with a fork, 9-12 minutes.

3. Meanwhile, mix together the remaining lemon juice, red cabbage, salsa, and sour cream in a medium bowl.
4. Put the cooked fish in a bowl, breaking it into large pieces. Then add the cabbage mixture, avocados, and warmed tortilla shells ready for assembly.
5. Enjoy!

Variations & Ingredients Tips:

▶ Use tilapia, mahi mahi or catfish instead of cod.
▶ Add some chopped jalapeños or hot sauce to the slaw for a kick.
▶ Serve with lime wedges, cilantro and sliced radishes.

Per serving: Calories: 370; Total Fat: 19g; Saturated Fat: 5g; Cholesterol: 75mg; Sodium: 620mg; Total Carbs: 27g; Dietary Fiber: 5g; Total Sugars: 4g; Protein: 29g

Fish Cakes

Servings: 4 | Prep Time: 20 Minutes | Cooking Time: 10 Minutes

Ingredients:

- 3/4 cup mashed potatoes (about 1 large russet potato)
- 340g cod or other white fish
- Salt and pepper
- Oil for misting or cooking spray
- 1 large egg
- 1/4 cup potato starch
- 1/2 cup panko breadcrumbs
- 1 tablespoon fresh chopped chives
- 2 tablespoons minced onion

Directions:

1. Peel potatoes, cut into cubes, and cook on stovetop till soft.
2. Salt and pepper raw fish to taste. Mist with oil or cooking spray, and cook in air fryer at 180°C/360°F for 6 to 8 minutes, until fish flakes easily. If fish is crowded, rearrange halfway through cooking to ensure all pieces cook evenly.
3. Transfer fish to a plate and break apart to cool.
4. Beat egg in a shallow dish.
5. Place potato starch in another shallow dish, and panko crumbs in a third dish.
6. When potatoes are done, drain in colander and rinse with cold water.
7. In a large bowl, mash the potatoes and stir in the chives and onion. Add salt and pepper to taste, then stir in the fish.
8. If needed, stir in a tablespoon of the beaten egg to help bind the mixture.
9. Shape into 8 small, fat patties. Dust lightly with potato starch, dip in egg, and roll in panko crumbs. Spray both sides with oil or cooking spray.
10. Cook at 180°C/360°F for 10 minutes, until golden brown and crispy.

Variations & Ingredients Tips:

▶ Add some lemon zest, capers or dill to the fish cake mixture.
▶ Use sweet potatoes instead of white for a different flavor.
▶ Serve with tartar sauce, aioli or malt vinegar.

Per serving: Calories: 240; Total Fat: 4g; Saturated Fat: 1g; Cholesterol: 95mg; Sodium: 230mg; Total Carbs: 28g; Dietary Fiber: 1g; Total Sugars: 1g; Protein: 22g

Old Bay Fish `n´ Chips

Servings: 4 | Prep Time: 20 Minutes | Cooking Time: 40 Minutes

Ingredients:

- 2 russet potatoes, peeled
- 2 tbsp olive oil
- 4 tilapia filets
- 1/4 cup flour
- Salt and pepper to taste
- 1 tsp Old Bay seasoning
- 1 lemon, zested
- 1 egg, beaten
- 1 cup panko bread crumbs
- 3 tbsp tartar sauce

Directions:

1. Preheat the air fryer to 200°C/400°F.
2. Slice the potatoes into 1.3cm-thick chips and drizzle with olive oil. Sprinkle with salt.
3. Add the fries to the frying basket and Air Fry for 12-16 minutes, shaking once. Remove to a plate. Cover loosely with foil.
4. Sprinkle the fish with salt and season with black pepper, lemon zest, and Old Bay seasoning, then lay on a plate.
5. Put the egg in a shallow bowl and spread the panko on a separate plate.
6. Dip the fish in the flour, then the egg, then the panko. Press to coat completely.
7. Add half the fish to the frying basket and spray with cooking oil. Set a raised rack on the basket, top with the other fish, and spray with cooking oil.
8. Air Fry for 8-10 minutes until the fish flakes.
9. Serve the fish and chips with tartar sauce.

Variations & Ingredients Tips:

- Use other firm white fish like cod or haddock.
- Make sweet potato fries or wedges instead of regular potato chips.
- Serve with lemon wedges and malt vinegar on the side.

Per serving: Calories 375, Total Fat 11g, Saturated Fat 2g, Cholesterol 130mg, Sodium 610mg, Total Carbs 48g, Fiber 3g, Sugars 2g, Protein 21g

Garlic-butter Lobster Tails

Servings: 2 | Prep Time: 5 Minutes | Cooking Time: 20 Minutes

Ingredients:

- 2 lobster tails
- 1 tbsp butter, melted
- 1/2 tsp Old Bay Seasoning
- 1/2 tsp garlic powder
- 1 tbsp chopped parsley
- 2 lemon wedges

Directions:

1. Preheat air fryer to 200°C/400°F.
2. Using kitchen shears, cut down the middle of each lobster tail on the softer side. Carefully run your finger between the lobster meat and the shell to loosen the meat.
3. Place lobster tails in the frying basket, cut sides up, and Air Fry for 4 minutes.
4. Rub with butter, garlic powder and Old Bay seasoning and cook for 4 more minutes.
5. Garnish with parsley and lemon wedges. Serve and enjoy!

Variations & Ingredients Tips:

- Add a pinch of cayenne or red pepper flakes for heat.
- Brush with a mixture of melted butter, lemon juice and Dijon mustard.
- Serve with drawn butter and steamed vegetables.

Per serving: Calories: 180; Total Fat: 8g; Saturated Fat: 4.5g; Cholesterol: 130mg; Sodium: 690mg; Total Carbs: 2g; Dietary Fiber: 0g; Total Sugars: 0g; Protein: 24g

British Fish & Chips

Servings: 4 | Prep Time: 20 Minutes | Cooking Time: 40 Minutes

Ingredients:

- 2 peeled russet potatoes, thinly sliced
- 1 egg white
- 1 tbsp lemon juice
- 1/3 cup ground almonds
- 2 bread slices, crumbled
- 1/2 tsp dried basil
- 4 haddock fillets

Directions:

1. Preheat air fryer to 200°C/390°F.
2. Lay the potato slices in the frying basket and Air Fry for 11-15 minutes. Turn the fries a couple of times while cooking.
3. While the fries are cooking, whisk the egg white and lemon juice together in a bowl. On a plate, combine the almonds, breadcrumbs, and basil.
4. First, one at a time, dip the fillets into the egg mix and then coat in the almond/breadcrumb mix. Lay the fillets on a wire rack until the fries are done.
5. Preheat the oven to 175°C/350°F. After the fries are done, move them to a pan and place in the oven to keep warm.
6. Put the fish in the frying basket and Air Fry for 10-14 minutes or until cooked through, golden, and crispy.
7. Serve with the fries.

Variations & Ingredients Tips:

- Use cod, pollock or halibut instead of haddock.
- Season the fish batter with salt, pepper and Old Bay seasoning.
- Serve with malt vinegar, tartar sauce and mushy peas.

Per serving: Calories: 400; Total Fat: 17g; Saturated Fat: 2g; Cholesterol: 80mg; Sodium: 260mg; Total Carbs: 34g; Dietary Fiber: 5g; Total Sugars: 2g; Protein: 31g

Maple Balsamic Glazed Salmon

Servings: 4 | Prep Time: 5 Minutes | Cooking Time: 10 Minutes

Ingredients:

- 4 (170g) fillets of salmon
- Salt and freshly ground black pepper
- Vegetable oil
- 1/4 cup pure maple syrup
- 3 tablespoons balsamic vinegar
- 1 teaspoon Dijon mustard

Directions:

1. Preheat the air fryer to 200°C/400°F.
2. Season the salmon well with salt and freshly ground black pepper. Spray or brush the bottom of the air fryer basket with vegetable oil and place the salmon fillets inside. Air-fry the salmon for 5 minutes.

3. While the salmon is air-frying, combine the maple syrup, balsamic vinegar and Dijon mustard in a small saucepan over medium heat and stir to blend well. Let the mixture simmer while the fish is cooking. It should start to thicken slightly, but keep your eye on it so it doesn't burn.
4. Brush the glaze on the salmon fillets and air-fry for an additional 5 minutes. The salmon should feel firm to the touch when finished and the glaze should be nicely browned on top. Brush a little more glaze on top before removing and serving with rice and vegetables, or a nice green salad.

Variations & Ingredients Tips:

- Substitute honey for the maple syrup if desired.
- Add a pinch of red pepper flakes to the glaze for some heat.
- Garnish with fresh thyme or parsley before serving.

Per serving: Calories: 330; Total Fat: 14g; Saturated Fat: 2g; Cholesterol: 95mg; Sodium: 130mg; Total Carbs: 18g; Dietary Fiber: 0g; Total Sugars: 14g; Protein: 33g

Californian Tilapia

Servings: 4 | Prep Time: 10 Minutes | Cooking Time: 15 Minutes

Ingredients:

- Salt and pepper to taste
- ¼ tsp garlic powder
- ¼ tsp chili powder
- ¼ tsp dried oregano
- ¼ tsp smoked paprika
- 1 tbsp butter, melted
- 4 tilapia fillets
- 2 tbsp lime juice
- 1 lemon, sliced

Directions:

1. Preheat air fryer to 200°C/400°F.
2. Combine salt, pepper, oregano, garlic powder, chili powder, and paprika in a small bowl.
3. Place tilapia in a pie pan, then pour lime juice and butter over the fish. Season both sides of the fish with the spice blend.
4. Arrange the tilapia in a single layer of the parchment-lined air fryer basket without touching each other.
5. Air Fry for 4 minutes, then carefully flip the fish. Air Fry for another 4 to 5 minutes until the fish is cooked and the outside is crispy.
6. Serve immediately with lemon slices on the side and enjoy.

Variations & Ingredients Tips:

- Substitute tilapia with cod, halibut, or snapper fillets.
- Add a sprinkle of grated Parmesan cheese or panko breadcrumbs before air frying for a crispy crust.
- Serve with avocado slices, pico de gallo, or a side of black beans and rice.

Per Serving: Calories: 160; Total Fat: 6g; Saturated Fat: 3g; Sodium: 200mg; Total Carbohydrates: 2g; Dietary Fiber: 0g; Total Sugars: 0g; Protein: 24g

Vegetarian Recipes

Easy Zucchini Lasagna Roll-ups

Servings: 2 | Prep Time: 20 Minutes | Cooking Time: 40 Minutes

Ingredients:
- 2 medium zucchini
- 2 tbsp lemon juice
- 1 ½ cups ricotta cheese
- 1 tbsp allspice
- 2 cups marinara sauce
- 1/3 cup mozzarella cheese

Directions:
1. Preheat air fryer to 200°C/400°F. Cut the ends of each zucchini, then slice into 6-mm thick pieces and drizzle with lemon juice. Roast for 5 minutes until slightly tender. Let cool slightly. Combine ricotta cheese and allspice in a bowl; set aside. Spread 2 tbsp of marinara sauce on the bottom of a baking pan. Spoon 1-2 tbsp of the ricotta mixture onto each slice, roll up each slice and place them spiral-side up in the pan. Scatter with the remaining ricotta mixture and drizzle with marinara sauce. Top with mozzarella cheese and Bake at 180°C/360°F for 20 minutes until the cheese is bubbly and golden brown. Serve warm.

Variations & Ingredients Tips:
- ▶ Substitute zucchini with eggplant or lasagna noodles for different textures.
- ▶ Add minced garlic, basil, or oregano to the ricotta mixture for extra flavor.
- ▶ Top with grated Parmesan cheese or breadcrumbs before baking for a crispy crust.

Per Serving: Calories: 470; Cholesterol: 80mg; Total Fat: 25g; Saturated Fat: 15g; Sodium: 1060mg; Total Carbohydrates: 38g; Dietary Fiber: 7g; Total Sugars: 22g; Protein: 29g

Fake Shepherd's Pie

Servings: 6 | Prep Time: 20 Minutes | Cooking Time: 40 Minutes

Ingredients:
- ½ head cauliflower, cut into florets
- 1 sweet potato, diced
- 1 tbsp olive oil
- ¼ cup cheddar shreds
- 2 tbsp milk
- Salt and pepper to taste
- 2 tsp avocado oil
- 1 cup beefless grounds
- ½ onion, diced
- 2 cloves garlic, minced
- 1 carrot, diced
- ½ cup green peas
- 1 stalk celery, diced
- 2/3 cup tomato sauce
- 1 tsp chopped rosemary
- 1 tsp thyme leaves

Directions:
1. Place cauliflower and sweet potato in a pot of salted boiling water over medium heat and simmer for 7 minutes until fork tender. Strain and transfer to a bowl. Put in avocado oil, cheddar, milk, salt and pepper. Mash until smooth.
2. Warm olive oil in a skillet over medium-high heat and stir in beefless grounds and vegetables and stir-fry for 4 minutes until veggies are tender. Stir in tomato sauce, rosemary, thyme, salt, and black pepper. Set aside.
3. Preheat air fryer to 175°C/350°F. Spoon filling into a round cake pan lightly greased with olive oil and cover with the topping. Using the tines of a fork, run shallow lines in the top of cauliflower for a decorative touch. Place cake pan in the frying basket and Air Fry for 12 minutes. Let sit for 10 minutes before serving.

Variations & Ingredients Tips:
- ▶ Use mashed potatoes instead of cauliflower and sweet potato for a more traditional topping.
- ▶ Substitute beefless grounds with cooked lentils or quinoa for a different protein option.
- ▶ Add Worcestershire sauce, soy sauce, or vegetable broth to the filling for extra savory flavor.

Per Serving: Calories: 220; Cholesterol: 10mg; Total Fat: 12g; Saturated Fat: 4g; Sodium: 520mg; Total Carbohydrates: 21g; Dietary Fiber: 5g; Total Sugars: 6g; Protein: 9g

Crunchy Rice Paper Samosas

Servings: 2 | Prep Time: 15 Minutes | Cooking Time: 20 Minutes

Ingredients:
- 1 boiled potato, mashed
- ¼ cup green peas
- 1 tsp garam masala powder
- ½ tsp ginger garlic paste
- ½ tsp cayenne pepper
- ½ tsp turmeric powder
- Salt and pepper to taste
- 3 rice paper wrappers

Directions:
1. Preheat air fryer to 175°C/350°F. Place the mashed pota-

toes in a bowl. Add the peas, garam masala powder, ginger garlic paste, cayenne pepper, turmeric powder, salt, and pepper and stir until ingredients are evenly blended.

2. Lay the rice paper wrappers out on a lightly floured surface. Divide the potato mixture between the wrappers and fold the top edges over to seal. Transfer the samosas to the greased frying basket and Air Fry for 12 minutes, flipping once until the samosas are crispy and flaky. Remove and leave to cool for 5 minutes. Serve and enjoy!

Variations & Ingredients Tips:

- Add finely chopped onions, carrots, or bell peppers to the potato mixture for extra veggies.
- Serve with mint chutney, tamarind chutney, or ketchup for dipping.
- Make a sweet version with mashed sweet potatoes, sugar, and cinnamon.

Per Serving: Calories: 210; Cholesterol: 0mg; Total Fat: 1g; Saturated Fat: 0g; Sodium: 330mg; Total Carbohydrates: 45g; Dietary Fiber: 4g; Total Sugars: 4g; Protein: 6g

Cheesy Veggie Frittata

Servings: 2 | Prep Time: 15 Minutes | Cooking Time: 65 Minutes

Ingredients:

- 115 grams Bella mushrooms, chopped
- ¼ cup halved grape tomatoes
- 1 cup baby spinach
- 1/3 cup chopped leeks
- 1 baby carrot, chopped
- 4 eggs
- ½ cup grated cheddar
- 1 tbsp milk
- ¼ tsp garlic powder
- ¼ tsp dried oregano
- Salt and pepper to taste

Directions:

1. Preheat air fryer to 150°C/300°F. Crack the eggs into a bowl and beat them with a fork or whisk. Mix in the remaining ingredients until well combined. Pour into a greased cake pan. Put the pan into the frying basket and Bake for 20-23 minutes or until eggs are set in the center. Remove from the fryer. Cut into halves and serve.

Variations & Ingredients Tips:

- Use different vegetables like bell peppers, zucchini, or asparagus for variety.
- Substitute cheddar with feta, goat cheese, or Parmesan for a different cheese flavor.
- Add cooked bacon, ham, or sausage for a non-vegetarian version.

Per Serving: Calories: 320; Cholesterol: 395mg; Total Fat: 21g; Saturated Fat: 10g; Sodium: 480mg; Total Carbohydrates: 11g; Dietary Fiber: 2g; Total Sugars: 5g; Protein: 24g

Eggplant Parmesan

Servings: 4 | Prep Time: 20 Minutes | Cooking Time: 8 Minutes Per Batch

Ingredients:

- 1 medium eggplant, 15-20 cm long
- salt
- 1 large egg
- 1 tablespoon water
- ⅔ cup panko breadcrumbs
- ⅓ cup grated Parmesan cheese, plus more for serving
- 1 tablespoon Italian seasoning
- ¾ teaspoon oregano
- oil for misting or cooking spray
- 1 680-gram jar marinara sauce
- 225 grams spaghetti, cooked
- pepper

Directions:

1. Preheat air fryer to 200°C/390°F.
2. Leaving peel intact, cut eggplant into 8 round slices about 2-cm thick. Salt to taste.
3. Beat egg and water in a shallow dish.
4. In another shallow dish, combine panko, Parmesan, Italian seasoning, and oregano.
5. Dip eggplant slices in egg wash and then crumbs, pressing lightly to coat.
6. Mist slices with oil or cooking spray.
7. Place 4 eggplant slices in air fryer basket and cook for 8 minutes, until brown and crispy.
8. While eggplant is cooking, heat marinara sauce.
9. Repeat step 7 to cook remaining eggplant slices.
10. To serve, place cooked spaghetti on plates and top with marinara and eggplant slices. At the table, pass extra Parmesan cheese and freshly ground black pepper.

Variations & Ingredients Tips:

- Substitute eggplant with zucchini or portobello mushrooms for a different veggie option.
- Use gluten-free breadcrumbs and pasta for a gluten-free version.
- Serve with a side salad or garlic bread for a complete meal.

Per Serving: Calories: 420; Cholesterol: 55mg; Total Fat: 11g; Saturated Fat: 3g; Sodium: 1180mg; Total Carbohydrates: 68g; Dietary Fiber: 9g; Total Sugars: 16g; Protein: 16g

Cheddar Bean Taquitos

Servings: 4 | Prep Time: 15 Minutes | Cooking Time: 25 Minutes

Ingredients:
- 1 cup refried beans
- 2 cups cheddar shreds
- ½ jalapeño pepper, minced
- ¼ chopped white onion
- 1 tsp oregano
- 15 soft corn tortillas

Directions:
1. Preheat air fryer at 175°C/350°F. Spread refried beans, jalapeño pepper, white onion, oregano and cheddar shreds down the center of each corn tortilla. Roll each tortilla tightly. Place tacos, seam side down, in the frying basket, and Air Fry for 4 minutes. Serve immediately.

Variations & Ingredients Tips:
- Substitute refried beans with black beans or pinto beans for a chunkier texture.
- Use flour tortillas instead of corn tortillas for a softer taquito.
- Serve with guacamole, pico de gallo, or Mexican crema for dipping.

Per Serving (about 4 taquitos): Calories: 510; Cholesterol: 60mg; Total Fat: 26g; Saturated Fat: 14g; Sodium: 860mg; Total Carbohydrates: 53g; Dietary Fiber: 8g; Total Sugars: 3g; Protein: 22g

Basil Green Beans

Servings: 4 | Prep Time: 5 Minutes | Cooking Time: 15 Minutes

Ingredients:
- 680 grams green beans, trimmed
- 1 tbsp olive oil
- 1 tbsp fresh basil, chopped
- Garlic salt to taste

Directions:
1. Preheat air fryer to 200°C/400°F. Coat the green beans with olive oil in a large bowl. Combine with fresh basil and garlic salt. Put the beans in the frying basket and Air Fry for 7-9 minutes, shaking once until the beans begin to brown. Serve warm and enjoy!

Variations & Ingredients Tips:
- Add sliced almonds or chopped bacon for extra crunch and flavor.
- Substitute basil with other fresh herbs like parsley, thyme, or oregano.
- Drizzle with balsamic vinegar or lemon juice before serving for a tangy twist.

Per Serving: Calories: 70; Cholesterol: 0mg; Total Fat: 4g; Saturated Fat: 0.5g; Sodium: 75mg; Total Carbohydrates: 9g; Dietary Fiber: 4g; Total Sugars: 4g; Protein: 2g

Home-style Cinnamon Rolls

Servings: 4 | Prep Time: 15 Minutes | Cooking Time: 40 Minutes

Ingredients:
- ½ pizza dough
- 1/3 cup dark brown sugar
- ¼ cup butter, softened
- ½ tsp ground cinnamon

Directions:
1. Preheat air fryer to 180°C/360°F.
2. Roll out the dough into a rectangle. Using a knife, spread the brown sugar and butter, covering all the edges, and sprinkle with cinnamon.
3. Fold the long side of the dough into a log, then cut it into 8 equal pieces, avoiding compression.
4. Place the rolls, spiral-side up, onto a parchment-lined sheet. Let rise for 20 minutes.
5. Grease the rolls with cooking spray and Bake for 8 minutes until golden brown.
6. Serve right away.

Variations & Ingredients Tips:
- Use store-bought pizza dough for a quicker preparation.
- Add chopped nuts like pecans or walnuts for extra crunch and flavor.
- Drizzle with a simple glaze made from powdered sugar and milk for added sweetness.

Per Serving: Calories: 280; Total Fat: 12g; Saturated Fat: 7g; Sodium: 320mg; Total Carbohydrates: 39g; Dietary Fiber: 1g; Total Sugars: 17g; Protein: 4g

Hearty Salad

Servings: 2 | Prep Time: 10 Minutes | Cooking Time: 15 Minutes

Ingredients:

Ingredients:

- 142 grams cauliflower, cut into florets
- 2 grated carrots
- 1 tbsp olive oil
- 1 tbsp lemon juice
- 2 tbsp raisins
- 2 tbsp roasted pepitas
- 2 tbsp diced red onion
- ¼ cup mayonnaise
- 1/8 tsp black pepper
- 1 tsp cumin
- ½ tsp chia seeds
- ½ tsp sesame seeds

Directions:

1. Preheat air fryer at 180°C/350°F.
2. Combine the cauliflower, cumin, olive oil, black pepper and lemon juice in a bowl, place it in the air fryer basket, and Bake for 5 minutes.
3. Transfer it to a serving dish. Toss in the remaining ingredients.
4. Let chill covered in the fridge until ready to use.
5. Serve sprinkled with sesame and chia seeds.

Variations & Ingredients Tips:

▶ Roast other vegetables like broccoli, bell peppers, or eggplant alongside the cauliflower.

▶ Use dried cranberries or chopped dates instead of raisins.

▶ Add chopped nuts like almonds or walnuts for extra crunch.

Per Serving: Calories: 310; Total Fat: 24g; Saturated Fat: 3.5g; Sodium: 220mg; Total Carbohydrates: 21g; Dietary Fiber: 6g; Total Sugars: 12g; Protein: 5g

Spiced Vegetable Galette

Servings: 4 | Prep Time: 15 Minutes | Cooking Time: 30 Minutes

Ingredients:

- ¼ cup cooked eggplant, chopped
- ¼ cup cooked zucchini, chopped
- 1 refrigerated pie crust
- 2 eggs
- ¼ cup milk
- Salt and pepper to taste
- 1 red chili, finely sliced
- ¼ cup tomato, chopped
- ½ cup shredded mozzarella cheese

Directions:

1. Preheat air fryer to 180°C/360°F.
2. In a baking dish, add the crust and press firmly. Trim off any excess edges. Poke a few holes.
3. Beat the eggs in a bowl. Stir in the milk, half of the cheese, eggplant, zucchini, tomato, red chili, salt, and pepper. Mix well.
4. Transfer the mixture to the baking dish and place in the air fryer.
5. Bake for 15 minutes or until firm and almost crusty. Slide the basket out and top with the remaining cheese.
6. Cook further for 5 minutes, or until golden brown. Let cool slightly and serve.

Variations & Ingredients Tips:

▶ Use puff pastry or phyllo dough instead of pie crust.

▶ Add sautéed onions, garlic, or mushrooms to the filling.

▶ Sprinkle with fresh herbs like basil, oregano, or thyme before serving.

Per Serving: Calories: 280; Total Fat: 18g; Saturated Fat: 7g; Sodium: 410mg; Total Carbohydrates: 21g; Dietary Fiber: 1g; Total Sugars: 4g; Protein: 9g

Sushi-style Deviled Eggs

Servings: 4 | Prep Time: 15 Minutes | Cooking Time: 20 Minutes

Ingredients:

- ¼ cup crabmeat, shells discarded
- 4 eggs
- 2 tbsp mayonnaise
- ½ tsp soy sauce
- ¼ avocado, diced
- ¼ tsp wasabi powder
- 2 tbsp diced cucumber
- 1 sheet nori, sliced
- 8 jarred pickled ginger slices
- 1 tsp toasted sesame seeds
- 2 spring onions, sliced

Directions:

1. Preheat air fryer to 130°C/260°F.
2. Place the eggs in muffin cups to avoid bumping around and cracking during the cooking process. Add silicone cups to the air fryer basket and Air Fry for 15 minutes.
3. Remove and plunge the eggs immediately into an ice bath to cool, about 5 minutes. Carefully peel and slice them in half lengthwise.
4. Spoon yolks into a separate medium bowl and arrange white halves on a large plate. Mash the yolks with a fork. Stir in mayonnaise, soy sauce, avocado, and wasabi powder until smooth. Mix in cucumber and spoon into white halves.
5. Scatter eggs with crabmeat, nori, pickled ginger, spring onions and sesame seeds to serve.

Variations & Ingredients Tips:

▶ Use smoked salmon or cooked shrimp instead of crabmeat.

- ▶ Add a drizzle of sriracha or hot sauce for extra heat.
- ▶ Garnish with furikake seasoning or bonito flakes.

Per Serving: Calories: 160; Total Fat: 12g; Saturated Fat: 3g; Sodium: 310mg; Total Carbohydrates: 4g; Dietary Fiber: 2g; Total Sugars: 1g; Protein: 10g

Tex-mex Potatoes With Avocado Dressing

Servings: 2 | Prep Time: 20 Minutes | Cooking Time: 60 Minutes

Ingredients:

- ¼ cup chopped parsley, dill, cilantro, chives
- ¼ cup yogurt
- ½ avocado, diced
- 2 tbsp milk
- 2 tsp lemon juice
- ½ tsp lemon zest
- 1 green onion, chopped
- 2 cloves garlic, quartered
- Salt and pepper to taste
- 2 tsp olive oil
- 2 russet potatoes, scrubbed and perforated with a fork
- 1 cup steamed broccoli florets
- ½ cup canned white beans

Directions:

1. In a food processor, blend the yogurt, avocado, milk, lemon juice, lemon zest, green onion, garlic, parsley, dill, cilantro, chives, salt and pepper until smooth. Transfer it to a small bowl and let chill the dressing covered in the fridge until ready to use.
2. Preheat air fryer at 200°C/400°F. Rub olive oil over both potatoes and sprinkle with salt and pepper. Place them in the air fryer basket and Bake for 45 minutes, flipping at 30 minutes mark.
3. Let cool onto a cutting board for 5 minutes until cool enough to handle. Cut each potato lengthwise into slices and pinch ends together to open up each slice.
4. Stuff broccoli and beans into potatoes and put them back into the basket, and cook for 3 more minutes.
5. Drizzle avocado dressing over and serve.

Variations & Ingredients Tips:

- ▶ Substitute russet potatoes with sweet potatoes or yams.
- ▶ Use cauliflower florets or asparagus instead of broccoli.
- ▶ Add cooked quinoa or brown rice to the stuffing.

Per Serving: Calories: 450; Total Fat: 18g; Saturated Fat: 3g; Sodium: 250mg; Total Carbohydrates: 64g; Dietary Fiber: 12g; Total Sugars: 5g; Protein: 14g

Cheesy Eggplant Rounds

Servings: 4 | Prep Time: 20 Minutes | Cooking Time: 35 Minutes

Ingredients:

- 1 eggplant, peeled
- 2 eggs
- ½ cup all-purpose flour
- ¾ cup breadcrumbs
- 2 tbsp grated Swiss cheese
- Salt and pepper to taste
- ¾ cup tomato passata
- ½ cup shredded Parmesan
- ½ cup shredded mozzarella

Directions:

1. Preheat air fryer to 200°C/400°F. Slice the eggplant into 25-cm rounds. Set aside. Set out three small bowls. In the first bowl, add flour. In the second bowl, beat the eggs. In the third bowl, mix the crumbs, 2 tbsp of grated Swiss cheese, salt, and pepper. Dip each eggplant in the flour, then dredge in egg, then coat with bread crumb mixture. Arrange the eggplant rounds on the greased frying basket and spray with cooking oil. Bake for 7 minutes. Top each eggplant round with 5 ml passata and ½ tbsp each of shredded Parmesan and mozzarella. Cook until the cheese melts, 2-3 minutes. Serve warm and enjoy!

Variations & Ingredients Tips:

- ▶ Use zucchini or summer squash instead of eggplant for a different vegetable option.
- ▶ Add minced garlic, basil, or oregano to the breadcrumb mixture for extra flavor.
- ▶ Serve with marinara sauce or pesto for dipping.

Per Serving: Calories: 280; Cholesterol: 115mg; Total Fat: 12g; Saturated Fat: 6g; Sodium: 620mg; Total Carbohydrates: 30g; Dietary Fiber: 5g; Total Sugars: 7g; Protein: 16g

Golden Breaded Mushrooms

Servings: 2 | Prep Time: 15 Minutes | Cooking Time: 20 Minutes

Ingredients:

- 2 cups crispy rice cereal
- 1 tsp nutritional yeast
- 2 tsp garlic powder
- 1 tsp dried oregano
- 1 tsp dried basil
- Salt to taste

- 1 tbsp Dijon mustard
- 1 tbsp mayonnaise
- 1/4 cup milk
- 225g whole mushrooms
- 4 tbsp chili sauce
- 3 tbsp mayonnaise

Directions:

1. Preheat air fryer at 175°C/350°F.
2. Blend rice cereal, garlic powder, oregano, basil, nutritional yeast, and salt in a food processor until it gets a breadcrumb consistency. Set aside in a bowl.
3. Mix the mustard, 1 tbsp mayonnaise, and milk in a bowl. Dip mushrooms in the mustard mixture; shake off excess. Then, dredge them in the breadcrumbs; shake off excess.
4. Place mushrooms in the greased frying basket and Air Fry for 7 minutes, shaking once.
5. Mix the 3 tbsp mayonnaise with chili sauce in a small bowl. Serve the mushrooms with the dipping sauce on the side.

Variations & Ingredients Tips:

▶ Use panko breadcrumbs instead of rice cereal for extra crunch.
▶ Add paprika or cayenne to the breading for a kick of spice.
▶ Stuff the mushroom caps with cheese or pesto before breading.

Per serving: Calories: 340; Total Fat: 20g; Saturated Fat: 3g; Sodium: 900mg; Total Carbs: 35g; Dietary Fiber: 3g; Total Sugars: 6g; Protein: 7g

Sweet Corn Bread

Servings: 6 | Prep Time: 10 Minutes | Cooking Time: 35 Minutes

Ingredients:

- 2 eggs, beaten
- ½ cup cornmeal
- ½ cup pastry flour
- 1/3 cup sugar
- 1 tsp lemon zest
- ½ tbsp baking powder
- ¼ tsp salt
- ¼ tsp baking soda
- ½ tbsp lemon juice
- ½ cup milk
- ¼ cup sunflower oil

Directions:

1. Preheat air fryer to 180°C/350°F.
2. Add the cornmeal, flour, sugar, lemon zest, baking powder, salt, and baking soda in a bowl. Stir with a whisk until combined.
3. Add the eggs, lemon juice, milk, and oil to another bowl and stir well. Add the wet mixture to the dry mixture and stir gently until combined.
4. Spray a baking pan with oil. Pour the batter in and Bake in the fryer for 25 minutes or until golden and a knife inserted in the center comes out clean.
5. Cut into wedges and serve.

Variations & Ingredients Tips:

▶ Add grated cheddar cheese, diced jalapeños, or corn kernels to the batter.
▶ Substitute lemon with orange or lime for a different citrus flavor.
▶ Serve with honey butter or maple syrup.

Per Serving: Calories: 240; Total Fat: 11g; Saturated Fat: 1.5g; Sodium: 290mg; Total Carbohydrates: 32g; Dietary Fiber: 1g; Total Sugars: 14g; Protein: 5g

Vegetarian Stuffed Bell Peppers

Servings: 3 | Prep Time: 15 Minutes | Cooking Time: 40 Minutes

Ingredients:

- 1 cup mushrooms, chopped
- 1 tbsp allspice
- 3/4 cup Alfredo sauce
- 1/2 cup canned diced tomatoes
- 1 cup cooked rice
- 2 tbsp dried parsley
- 2 tbsp hot sauce
- Salt and pepper to taste
- 3 large bell peppers

Directions:

1. Preheat air fryer to 190°C/375°F.
2. Whisk mushrooms, allspice and 1 cup of boiling water until smooth.
3. Stir in Alfredo sauce, tomatoes and juices, rice, parsley, hot sauce, salt, and black pepper. Set aside.
4. Cut the top of each bell pepper, take out the core and seeds without breaking the pepper.
5. Fill each pepper with the rice mixture and cover them with a 15-cm square of aluminum foil, folding the edges.
6. Roast for 30 minutes until tender.
7. Let cool completely before unwrapping. Serve immediately.

Variations & Ingredients Tips:

▶ Use different grains like quinoa or farro instead of rice.
▶ Add vegan cheese shreds to the filling.
▶ Top with vegan sour cream or cashew cream.

Per Serving: Calories: 316; Total Fat: 14g; Saturated Fat: 3g; Sodium: 1156mg; Total Carbohydrates: 42g; Dietary Fiber: 5g; Total Sugars: 10g; Protein: 8g

Stuffed Zucchini Boats

Servings: 2 | Prep Time: 15 Minutes | Cooking Time: 20 Minutes

Ingredients:

- Olive oil
- 1/2 cup onion, finely chopped
- 1 clove garlic, finely minced
- 1/2 teaspoon dried oregano
- 1/4 teaspoon dried thyme
- 3/4 cup couscous
- 1 1/2 cups chicken stock, divided
- 1 tomato, seeds removed and finely chopped
- 1/2 cup coarsely chopped Kalamata olives
- 1/2 cup grated Romano cheese
- 1/4 cup pine nuts, toasted
- 1 tablespoon chopped fresh parsley
- 1 teaspoon salt
- Freshly ground black pepper
- 1 egg, beaten
- 1 cup grated mozzarella cheese, divided
- 2 thick zucchini

Directions:

1. Sauté onion, garlic, oregano and thyme in olive oil.
2. Add couscous and 1 1/4 cups stock. Simmer until absorbed.
3. Fluff couscous and add tomato, olives, Romano, pine nuts, parsley, salt and pepper.
4. Mix in remaining stock, egg and 1/2 cup mozzarella.
5. Cut zucchini in half, trim to 13-cm lengths and hollow out.
6. Brush with oil, season with salt and pepper.
7. Preheat air fryer to 195°C/380°F.
8. Fill zucchini with couscous mixture and mound high.
9. Air fry for 19 minutes. Top with remaining mozzarella and cook 1 more minute.
10. Garnish with parsley.

Variations & Ingredients Tips:

- Use quinoa or bulgur instead of couscous.
- Omit olives and add roasted red peppers.
- Top with vegan parmesan for dairy-free version.

Per Serving: Calories: 586; Total Fat: 29g; Saturated Fat: 11g; Sodium: 1452mg; Total Carbohydrates: 58g; Dietary Fiber: 6g; Total Sugars: 10g; Protein: 25g

Veggie-stuffed Bell Peppers

Servings: 4 | Prep Time: 15 Minutes | Cooking Time: 40 Minutes

Ingredients:

- 1/2 cup canned fire-roasted diced tomatoes, including juice
- 2 red bell peppers
- 4 tsp olive oil
- 1/2 yellow onion, diced
- 1 zucchini, diced
- 3/4 cup chopped mushrooms
- 1/4 cup tomato sauce
- 2 tsp Italian seasoning
- 1/4 tsp smoked paprika
- Salt and pepper to taste

Directions:

1. Cut bell peppers in half from top to bottom and discard the seeds. Brush inside and tops of the bell peppers with some olive oil. Set aside.
2. Warm the remaining olive oil in a skillet over medium heat. Stir-fry the onion, zucchini, and mushrooms for 5 minutes until the onions are tender.
3. Combine tomatoes and their juice, tomato sauce, Italian seasoning, paprika, salt, and pepper in a bowl.
4. Preheat air fryer to 180°C/350°F.
5. Divide both mixtures between bell pepper halves.
6. Place bell pepper halves in the frying basket and Air Fry for 8 minutes.
7. Serve immediately.

Variations & Ingredients Tips:

- Add cooked grains like quinoa or rice for extra protein and fiber.
- Use different cheese like vegan feta or cheddar shreds
- Substitute bell peppers with portobello mushroom caps.

Per Serving: Calories: 113; Total Fat: 6g; Saturated Fat: 1g; Sodium: 179mg; Total Carbohydrates: 13g; Dietary Fiber: 4g; Total Sugars: 7g; Protein: 3g

Sesame Orange Tofu With Snow Peas

Servings: 4 | Prep Time: 20 Minutes | Cooking Time: 40 Minutes

Ingredients:

- 400 grams tofu, cubed
- 1 tbsp tamari
- 1 tsp olive oil
- 1 tsp sesame oil

- 1 ½ tbsp cornstarch, divided
- ½ tsp salt
- ¼ tsp garlic powder
- 1 cup snow peas
- ½ cup orange juice
- ¼ cup vegetable broth
- 1 orange, zested
- 1 garlic clove, minced
- ¼ tsp ground ginger
- 2 scallions, chopped
- 1 tbsp sesame seeds
- 2 cups cooked jasmine rice
- 2 tbsp chopped parsley

Directions:

1. Preheat air fryer to 200°C/400°F.
2. Combine tofu, tamari, olive oil, and sesame oil in a large bowl until tofu is coated. Add in 1 tablespoon cornstarch, salt, and garlic powder and toss.
3. Arrange the tofu on the air fryer basket. Air Fry for 5 minutes, then shake the basket. Add snow peas and Air Fry for 5 minutes. Place tofu mixture in a bowl.
4. Bring the orange juice, vegetable broth, orange zest, garlic, and ginger to a boil over medium heat in a small saucepan. Whisk the rest of the cornstarch and 1 tablespoon water in a small bowl to make a slurry. Pour the slurry into the saucepan and constantly stir for 2 minutes until the sauce has thickened. Let off the heat for 2 minutes.
5. Pour the orange sauce, scallions, and sesame seeds in the bowl with the tofu and stir to coat.
6. Serve with jasmine rice sprinkled with parsley. Enjoy!

Variations & Ingredients Tips:

- ▶ Use tempeh or seitan instead of tofu for a different texture.
- ▶ Add sliced bell peppers, mushrooms, or carrots to the stir-fry.
- ▶ Serve over quinoa, brown rice, or rice noodles for variation.

Per Serving: Calories: 360; Total Fat: 14g; Saturated Fat: 2g; Sodium: 610mg; Total Carbohydrates: 45g; Dietary Fiber: 4g; Total Sugars: 8g; Protein: 16g

Two-cheese Grilled Sandwiches

Servings: 2 | Prep Time: 10 Minutes | Cooking Time: 30 Minutes

Ingredients:

- 4 sourdough bread slices
- 2 cheddar cheese slices
- 2 Swiss cheese slices
- 1 tbsp butter
- 2 dill pickles, sliced

Directions:

1. Preheat air fryer to 180°C/360°F.
2. Smear both sides of the sourdough bread with butter and place them in the air fryer basket. Toast the bread for 6 minutes, flipping once.
3. Divide the cheddar cheese between 2 of the bread slices. Cover the remaining 2 bread slices with Swiss cheese slices.
4. Bake for 10 more minutes until the cheeses have melted and lightly bubbled and the bread has golden brown.
5. Set the cheddar-covered bread slices on a serving plate, cover with pickles, and top each with the Swiss-covered slices.
6. Serve and enjoy!

Variations & Ingredients Tips:

- ▶ Use different types of cheese like provolone, Gruyere, or Monterey Jack.
- ▶ Add sliced tomatoes, avocado, or bacon for extra flavor and texture.
- ▶ Serve with a side of mustard or mayonnaise for dipping.

Per Serving: Calories: 470; Total Fat: 29g; Saturated Fat: 17g; Sodium: 960mg; Total Carbohydrates: 34g; Dietary Fiber: 2g; Total Sugars: 2g; Protein: 22g

Vegetable Side Dishes Recipes

Southern Okra Chips

Servings: 2 | Prep Time: 10 Minutes | Cooking Time: 20 Minutes

Ingredients:
- 2 eggs
- 60 ml whole milk
- 60 ml bread crumbs
- 60 ml cornmeal
- 1 tablespoon Cajun seasoning
- Salt and pepper to taste
- 1/8 teaspoon chili pepper
- 225 g okra, sliced
- 1 tablespoon butter, melted

Directions:
1. Preheat air fryer at 200°C/400°F.
2. Beat the eggs and milk in a bowl.
3. In another bowl, combine the remaining ingredients, except okra and butter.
4. Dip okra chips in the egg mixture, then dredge them in the breadcrumbs mixture.
5. Place okra chips in the greased frying basket and Roast for 7 minutes, shake once and brush with melted butter.
6. Serve right away.

Variations & Ingredients Tips:
- Use panko breadcrumbs or crushed crackers instead of regular breadcrumbs for a crunchier texture.
- Add some grated Parmesan cheese or nutritional yeast to the breadcrumb mixture for a cheesy flavor.
- Serve the okra chips with a dipping sauce, such as ranch dressing or remoulade sauce.

Per Serving: Calories: 320; Total Fat: 16g; Saturated Fat: 6g; Cholesterol: 205mg; Sodium: 840mg; Total Carbs: 33g; Fiber: 4g; Sugars: 5g; Protein: 13g

Crispy Herbed Potatoes

Servings: 6 | Prep Time: 10 Minutes | Cooking Time: 20 Minutes

Ingredients:
- 3 medium baking potatoes, washed and cubed
- 1/2 teaspoon dried thyme
- 1 teaspoon minced dried rosemary
- 1/2 teaspoon garlic powder
- 1 teaspoon sea salt
- 1/2 teaspoon black pepper
- 2 tablespoons extra-virgin olive oil
- 1/4 cup chopped parsley

Directions:
1. Preheat the air fryer to 198°C/390°F.
2. Pat the potatoes dry. In a bowl, mix the cubed potatoes with thyme, rosemary, garlic powder, salt, pepper.
3. Drizzle and toss with olive oil.
4. Pour the herbed potatoes into the air fryer basket. Cook for 20 minutes, stirring every 5 minutes.
5. Toss the cooked potatoes with chopped parsley and serve immediately.

Variations & Ingredients Tips:
- Use sweet potatoes instead of russet.
- Add chili powder, paprika or cayenne for a spicy kick.
- Toss with freshly grated parmesan before serving.

Per Serving: Calories 140; Total Fat 4g; Saturated Fat 1g; Cholesterol 0mg; Sodium 440mg; Total Carbs 23g; Fiber 3g; Sugars 1g; Protein 3g

Roasted Corn Salad

Servings: 3 | Prep Time: 10 Minutes | Cooking Time: 15 Minutes

Ingredients:
- 3 (10cm) lengths husked and de-silked corn on the cob
- Olive oil spray
- 1 cup packed baby arugula leaves
- 12 cherry tomatoes, halved
- Up to 3 medium scallions, trimmed and thinly sliced
- 2 tablespoons lemon juice
- 1 tablespoon olive oil
- 1 1/2 teaspoons honey
- 1/4 teaspoon mild paprika
- 1/4 teaspoon dried oregano
- 1/4 teaspoon + more to taste table salt
- 1/4 teaspoon ground black pepper

Directions:
1. Preheat air fryer to 204°C/400°F.
2. Coat corn cobs lightly with olive oil spray. Place in air fryer basket, spaced apart. Air fry 15 minutes until charred in spots.
3. Let corn cool 15 minutes. Cut kernels off the cobs.
4. In a bowl, combine corn kernels, chopped arugula, tomatoes and scallions.
5. Make dressing by whisking lemon juice, olive oil, hon-

ey, paprika, oregano, salt and pepper.
6. Pour dressing over salad and toss to coat. Season with more salt if needed.

Variations & Ingredients Tips:

▶ Use grilled corn if not in season.

▶ Add crumbled feta or diced avocado.

▶ Substitute lime juice for the lemon juice in the dressing.

Per Serving: 152 Calories; 6g Total Fat; 1g Saturated Fat; 0mg Cholesterol; 119mg Sodium; 24g Total Carbs; 4g Fiber; 9g Sugars; 4g Protein

Mediterranean Roasted Vegetables

Servings: 4 | Prep Time: 10 Minutes | Cooking Time: 30 Minutes

Ingredients:

- 1 red bell pepper, cut into chunks
- 1 cup sliced mushrooms
- 1 cup green beans, diced
- 1 zucchini, sliced
- 1/3 cup diced red onion
- 3 garlic cloves, sliced
- 2 tbsp olive oil
- 1 tsp rosemary
- 1/2 tsp flaked sea salt

Directions:

1. Preheat air fryer to 177°C/350°F.
2. Add the bell pepper, mushrooms, green beans, red onion, zucchini, rosemary, and garlic to a bowl and mix.
3. Spritz with olive oil and stir until well-coated.
4. Put the veggies in the frying basket and air fry for 14-18 minutes until crispy and softened.
5. Serve sprinkled with flaked sea salt.

Variations & Ingredients Tips:

▶ Add diced eggplant or cherry tomatoes.

▶ Use balsamic vinegar instead of olive oil.

▶ Toss with fresh basil or parmesan after cooking.

Per Serving: 88 Calories; 5g Total Fat; 1g Saturated Fat; 0mg Cholesterol; 106mg Sodium; 10g Total Carbs; 3g Fiber; 5g Sugars; 3g Protein

Steak Fries

Servings: 4 | Prep Time: 5 Minutes | Cooking Time: 25 Minutes

Ingredients:

- 900 g Medium Yukon Gold or other yellow potatoes (peeled or not—your choice)
- 2 tablespoons olive oil
- ½ teaspoon, or more to taste table salt
- ½ teaspoon, or more to taste ground black pepper

Directions:

1. Preheat the air fryer to 180°C/350°F.
2. Cut the potatoes lengthwise into wedges about 5 cm wide at the outer edge. Toss these wedges in a bowl with the oil, salt, and pepper until the wedges are evenly coated in the oil. (Start with the minimum amounts of salt and pepper we recommend—you can always add more later.)
3. When the machine is at temperature, set the wedges in the basket in a crisscross stack, with about half of the wedges first lining in the basket's bottom, then others set on top of those at a 45-degree angle. Air-fry undisturbed for 15 minutes.
4. Increase the machine's temperature to 200°C/400°F. Toss the fries so they're no longer in a crisscross pattern but more like a mound. Air-fry for 10 minutes more (from the moment you raise the temperature), tossing and rearranging the fries once, until they're crisp and brown.
5. Pour them onto a wire rack and cool for a few minutes before serving hot.

Variations & Ingredients Tips:

▶ Try using sweet potatoes or russet potatoes for a different flavor and texture.

▶ Season the fries with garlic powder, onion powder, paprika, or your favorite spice blend before cooking.

▶ Serve the fries with ketchup, mayo, or your favorite dipping sauce.

Per Serving: Calories: 230; Total Fat: 7g; Saturated Fat: 1g; Cholesterol: 0mg; Sodium: 300mg; Total Carbs: 38g; Fiber: 4g; Sugars: 1g; Protein: 4g

Balsamic Beet Chips

Servings: 4 | Prep Time: 10 Minutes | Cooking Time: 40 Minutes

Ingredients:

- ½ tsp balsamic vinegar
- 4 beets, peeled and sliced
- 1 garlic clove, minced
- 2 tbsp chopped mint
- Salt and pepper to taste
- 3 tbsp olive oil

Directions:

1. Preheat air fryer to 193°C/380°F.
2. Coat all ingredients in a bowl, except balsamic vinegar.
3. Pour the beet mixture into the frying basket and Roast for 25-30 minutes, stirring once.
4. Serve, drizzled with vinegar and enjoy!

Variations & Ingredients Tips:

▶ Use different fresh herbs like rosemary or thyme.

▶ Toss with parmesan cheese before cooking.

▶ Sprinkle with smoked paprika or cumin after cooking.

Per Serving: Calories 125; Total Fat 9g; Saturated Fat 1g; Cholesterol 0mg; Sodium 125mg; Total Carbs 10g; Fiber 2g; Sugars 8g; Protein 1g

Pork Tenderloin Salad

Servings: 4 | Prep Time: 15 Minutes | Cooking Time: 25 Minutes

Ingredients:

- Pork Tenderloin:
- 1/2 teaspoon smoked paprika
- 1/4 teaspoon salt
- 1/4 teaspoon garlic powder
- 1/2 teaspoon onion powder
- 1/8 teaspoon ginger
- 1 teaspoon extra-light olive oil
- 340g pork tenderloin
- Dressing:
- 3 tablespoons extra-light olive oil
- 2 tablespoons red wine vinegar
- 2 tablespoons Dijon mustard
- 1 tablespoon honey
- Salad:
- 1/4 sweet red bell pepper
- 1 large Granny Smith apple
- 8 cups shredded napa cabbage

Directions:

1. Mix tenderloin seasonings with oil and rub over pork.
2. Place tenderloin in air fryer basket and cook at 199°C/390°F for 25 mins until 54°C/130°F internal temp.
3. Let meat rest while preparing salad and dressing.
4. Make dressing by shaking all ingredients in a jar until mixed.
5. Cut bell pepper into strips, core and slice apple.
6. Toss cabbage, pepper, apple and dressing in a bowl.
7. Divide salad among plates and top with sliced pork tenderloin.
8. Serve with veggie chips.

Variations & Ingredients Tips:

▶ Use chicken breast or beef tenderloin instead of pork.

▶ Add crumbled feta, walnuts or dried cranberries to the salad.

▶ Serve the tenderloin over mashed potatoes or rice instead.

Per Serving: 310 Calories; 14g Total Fat; 3g Saturated Fat; 63mg Cholesterol; 403mg Sodium; 26g Total Carbs; 5g Fiber; 16g Sugars; 21g Protein

Wilted Brussels Sprout Slaw

Servings: 4 | Prep Time: 10 Minutes | Cooking Time: 18 Minutes

Ingredients:

- 2 thick-cut bacon strips, halved widthwise (gluten-free, if a concern)
- 570 g bagged shredded Brussels sprouts
- 1/4 tsp table salt
- 2 tbsp white balsamic vinegar (see here)
- 2 tsp Worcestershire sauce (gluten-free, if a concern)
- 1 tsp Dijon mustard (gluten-free, if a concern)
- 1/4 tsp ground black pepper

Directions:

1. Preheat the air fryer to 190°C/375°F. When the machine is at temperature, lay the bacon strip halves in the basket in one layer and air-fry for 10 minutes, or until crisp. Use kitchen tongs to transfer the bacon pieces to a wire rack. Put the shredded Brussels sprouts in a large bowl. Drain any fat from the basket or the tray under the basket onto the Brussels sprouts. Add the salt and toss well to coat. Put the Brussels sprout shreds in the basket, spreading them out into as close to an even layer as you can. Air-fry for 8 minutes, tossing the basket's contents at least three times, until wilted and lightly browned. Pour the contents of the basket into a serving bowl. Chop the bacon and add it to the Brussels sprouts. Add the vinegar, Worcestershire sauce, mustard, and pepper. Toss well to blend the dressing and coat the Brussels sprout shreds. Serve warm.

Variations & Ingredients Tips:

▶ Add chopped apples, dried cranberries, or toasted pecans for a sweet and crunchy twist.

▶ Sprinkle with grated Parmesan cheese or nutritional yeast before serving for a cheesy flavor.

▶ Use kale, cabbage, or a mix of greens instead of Brussels sprouts for a different slaw base.

Per Serving: Calories: 117; Total Fat: 5g; Saturated Fat: 2g; Cholesterol: 10mg; Sodium: 342mg; Total Carbohydrates: 12g; Dietary Fiber: 5g; Total

Sugars: 3g; Protein: 7g

Mom's Potatoes Au Gratin

Servings: 4 | Prep Time: 15 Minutes | Cooking Time: 50 Minutes

Ingredients:

- 4 Yukon gold potatoes, peeled
- 1 cup shredded cheddar cheese
- 2 tbsp grated Parmesan cheese
- 2 garlic cloves, minced
- 1/3 cup heavy cream
- 1/3 cup whole milk
- 1/2 tsp dried marjoram
- Salt and pepper to taste

Directions:

1. Preheat the air fryer to 177°C/350°F. Spray a 17cm round pan with cooking oil.
2. Cut the potatoes into 3mm-thick slices and layer in the pan along with cheddar cheese and garlic.
3. Mix the cream, milk, marjoram, salt, and pepper in a bowl, then pour over the potatoes.
4. Sprinkle with Parmesan and place pan in air fryer basket.
5. Bake for 25-35 minutes until potatoes are tender, sauce is bubbling and top is golden.
6. Serve warm.

Variations & Ingredients Tips:

- Add cooked bacon or ham between the potato layers.
- Use a blend of cheeses like gruyere and parmesan.
- Top with breadcrumbs before baking for a crunchy topping.

Per Serving: 303 Calories; 17g Total Fat; 10g Saturated Fat; 53mg Cholesterol; 220mg Sodium; 30g Total Carbs; 3g Fiber; 4g Sugars; 10g Protein

Acorn Squash Halves With Maple Butter Glaze

Servings: 2 | Prep Time: 10 Minutes | Cooking Time: 33 Minutes

Ingredients:

- 1 medium (454g to 567g) Acorn squash
- Vegetable oil spray
- 1/4 teaspoon Table salt
- 1½ tablespoons Butter, melted
- 1½ tablespoons Maple syrup

Directions:

1. Preheat the air fryer to 162°C/325°F (or 166°C/330°F, if that's the closest setting).
2. Cut a squash in half through the stem end. Use a flatware spoon (preferably, a serrated grapefruit spoon) to scrape out and discard the seeds and membranes in each half. Use a paring knife to make a crisscross pattern of cuts about 1.3 cm apart and 0.6 cm deep across the "meat" of the squash. If working with a second squash, repeat this step for that one.
3. Generously coat the cut side of the squash halves with vegetable oil spray. Sprinkle the halves with the salt. Set them in the basket cut side up with at least 0.6 cm between them. Air-fry undisturbed for 30 minutes.
4. Increase the machine's temperature to 204°C/400°F. Mix the melted butter and syrup in a small bowl until uniform. Brush this mixture over the cut sides of the squash(es), letting it pool in the center. Air-fry undisturbed for 3 minutes, or until the glaze is bubbling.
5. Use a nonstick-safe spatula and kitchen tongs to transfer the squash halves cut side up to a wire rack. Cool for 5 to 10 minutes before serving.

Variations & Ingredients Tips:

▶ Substitute brown sugar for the maple syrup for a different flavor profile.

▶ Add chopped pecans or walnuts to the glaze for crunch.

▶ Sprinkle with cinnamon or pumpkin pie spice before glazing.

Per Serving: Calories 207; Total Fat 9g; Saturated Fat 5g; Cholesterol 20mg; Sodium 230mg; Total Carbs 33g; Fiber 3g; Sugars 12g; Protein 2g

Best-ever Brussels Sprouts

Servings: 4 | Prep Time: 5 Minutes | Cooking Time: 30 Minutes

Ingredients:

- 455g Brussels sprouts, halved lengthwise
- 2 tbsp olive oil
- 3 tsp chili powder
- 1 tbsp lemon juice

Directions:

1. Preheat air fryer to 198°C/390°F.
2. Add the sprouts in a bowl, drizzle with olive oil and 2 tsp of chili powder, and toss to coat.
3. Set them in the frying basket and Air Fry for 12 minutes. Shake at least once.
4. Season with the remaining chili powder and lemon

juice, shake once again, and cook for 3-5 minutes until golden and crispy.
5. Serve warm.

Variations & Ingredients Tips:

▶ Use smoked paprika instead of regular chili powder.
▶ Toss with grated parmesan before serving.
▶ Drizzle with balsamic glaze after cooking.

Per Serving: Calories 110; Total Fat 7g; Saturated Fat 1g; Cholesterol 0mg; Sodium 220mg; Total Carbs 10g; Fiber 4g; Sugars 3g; Protein 4g

Dilly Sesame Roasted Asparagus

Servings: 6 | Prep Time: 5 Minutes | Cooking Time: 15 Minutes

Ingredients:

- 454g asparagus, trimmed
- 1 tbsp butter, melted
- ¼ tsp salt
- 1 clove garlic, minced
- 2 tsp chopped dill
- 3 tbsp sesame seeds

Directions:

1. Preheat air fryer to 188°C/370°F.
2. Combine asparagus and butter in a bowl.
3. Place asparagus mixture in the frying basket and Roast for 9 minutes, tossing once.
4. Transfer it to a serving dish and stir in salt, garlic, sesame seeds and dill until coated.
5. Serve immediately.

Variations & Ingredients Tips:

▶ Use olive oil instead of butter.
▶ Add lemon zest or red pepper flakes for extra zing.
▶ Substitute parsley or chives for the dill.

Per Serving: Calories 75; Total Fat 5g; Saturated Fat 2g; Cholesterol 7mg; Sodium 95mg; Total Carbs 5g; Fiber 2g; Sugars 2g; Protein 3g

Herbed Zucchini Poppers

Servings: 4 | Prep Time: 10 Minutes | Cooking Time: 30 Minutes

Ingredients:

- 1 tbsp grated Parmesan cheese
- 2 zucchini, sliced
- 1 cup breadcrumbs
- 2 eggs, beaten
- Salt and pepper to taste
- 1 tsp dry tarragon
- 1 tsp dry dill

Directions:

1. Preheat air fryer to 199°C/390°F.
2. Place the breadcrumbs, Parmesan, tarragon, dill, salt, and pepper in a bowl and stir to combine.
3. Dip the zucchini into the beaten eggs, then coat with Parmesan-crumb mixture.
4. Lay the zucchini slices on the greased frying basket in an even layer.
5. Air fry for 14-16 minutes, shaking the basket several times during cooking.
6. When ready, the zucchini will be crispy and golden brown.
7. Serve hot and enjoy!

Variations & Ingredients Tips:

▶ Use panko breadcrumbs for extra crispiness.
▶ Substitute parmesan for breadcrumbs for a low-carb version.
▶ Add garlic powder or Italian seasoning to the breadcrumb mix.

Per Serving: 190 Calories; 6g Total Fat; 2g Saturated Fat; 107mg Cholesterol; 530mg Sodium; 26g Total Carbs; 3g Fiber; 4g Sugars; 9g Protein

Tandoori Cauliflower

Servings: 4 | Prep Time: 10 Minutes | Cooking Time: 10 Minutes

Ingredients:

- 120 ml plain full-fat yogurt (not Greek yogurt)
- 7.5 ml yellow curry powder, purchased or homemade
- 7.5 ml lemon juice
- 3.75 ml table salt (optional)
- 1.125 L (about 500 g) cauliflower florets, cut into 5 cm pieces

Directions:

1. Preheat the air fryer to 200°C/400°F.
2. Whisk the yogurt, curry powder, lemon juice, and salt (if using) in a large bowl until uniform. Add the florets and stir gently to coat the florets well and evenly. Even better, use your clean, dry hands to get the yogurt mixture down into all the nooks of the florets.
3. When the machine is at temperature, transfer the florets to the basket, spreading them gently into as close to one layer as you can. Air-fry for 10 minutes, tossing and rearranging the florets twice so that any covered or touch-

ing parts are exposed to the air currents, until lightly browned and tender if still a bit crunchy.

4. Pour the contents of the basket onto a wire rack. Cool for at least 5 minutes before serving, or serve at room temperature.

Variations & Ingredients Tips:

- ▶ Use different types of curry powder, such as Madras or garam masala, for a variety of flavors.
- ▶ Add some minced garlic or ginger to the yogurt mixture for extra flavor.
- ▶ Serve the cauliflower with a dipping sauce, such as cilantro chutney or raita.

Per Serving: Calories: 70; Total Fat: 2.5g; Saturated Fat: 1.5g; Cholesterol: 5mg; Sodium: 170mg; Total Carbs: 9g; Fiber: 3g; Sugars: 4g; Protein: 4g

Steakhouse Baked Potatoes

Servings: 3 | Prep Time: 5 Minutes | Cooking Time: 55 Minutes

Ingredients:

- 3 russet potatoes (280 g each)
- 2 tablespoons olive oil
- 1 teaspoon table salt

Directions:

1. Preheat the air fryer to 190°C/375°F.
2. Poke holes all over each potato with a fork. Rub the skin of each potato with 2 teaspoons of the olive oil, then sprinkle ¼ teaspoon salt all over each potato.
3. When the machine is at temperature, set the potatoes in the basket in one layer with as much air space between them as possible. Air-fry for 50 minutes, turning once, or until soft to the touch but with crunchy skins. If the machine is at 180°C/360°F, you may need to add up to 5 minutes to the cooking time.
4. Use kitchen tongs to gently transfer the baked potatoes to a wire rack. Cool for 5 or 10 minutes before serving.

Variations & Ingredients Tips:

- ▶ Try using different types of potatoes, such as Yukon Gold or red potatoes, for a different flavor and texture.
- ▶ Top the baked potatoes with your favorite toppings, such as butter, sour cream, cheese, bacon bits, or chives.
- ▶ For a healthier version, use a small amount of olive oil or skip the oil altogether and wrap the potatoes in foil before cooking.

Per Serving: Calories: 280; Total Fat: 7g; Saturated Fat: 1g; Cholesterol: 0mg; Sodium: 800mg; Total Carbs: 50g; Fiber: 4g; Sugars: 2g; Protein: 6g

Honey-mustard Roasted Cabbage

Servings: 4 | Prep Time: 10 Minutes | Cooking Time: 35 Minutes

Ingredients:

- 4 cups chopped green cabbage
- 1/3 cup honey mustard dressing
- 1 shallot, chopped
- 2 garlic cloves, minced
- 2 tbsp olive oil
- 1 tbsp lemon juice
- 1 tbsp cornstarch
- 1/2 tsp fennel seeds

Directions:

1. Preheat the air fryer to 188°C/370°F.
2. Toss the cabbage, shallot, olive oil and garlic in a cake pan.
3. Bake for 10 minutes or until the cabbage is wilted, then drain the excess liquid.
4. While cabbage is cooking, combine the salad dressing, lemon juice, cornstarch, and fennel seeds in a bowl.
5. Take pan out and pour out excess liquid. Pour the dressing mix over the drained cabbage and mix well.
6. Return pan to fryer and bake for 7-11 minutes more, stirring twice, until cabbage is tender and sauce has thickened.
7. Serve warm.

Variations & Ingredients Tips:

- ▶ Use red or savoy cabbage for different flavors.
- ▶ Add bacon or pancetta for a smoky flavor.
- ▶ Substitute apple cider vinegar for the lemon juice.

Per Serving: 155 Calories; 10g Total Fat; 1g Saturated Fat; 1mg Cholesterol; 312mg Sodium; 16g Total Carbs; 4g Fiber; 9g Sugars; 2g Protein

Mushrooms, Sautéed

Servings: 4 | Prep Time: 5 Minutes | Cooking Time: 4 Minutes

Ingredients:

- 227g sliced white mushrooms, rinsed and well drained

- 1/4 teaspoon garlic powder
- 1 tablespoon Worcestershire sauce

Directions:

1. Place mushrooms in a large bowl and sprinkle with garlic powder and Worcestershire sauce. Stir well to distribute seasonings evenly.
2. Place in air fryer basket and cook at 199°C/390°F for 4 minutes, until tender.

Variations & Ingredients Tips:

- ▶ Add a pat of butter or olive oil for extra richness.
- ▶ Use a blend of mushroom varieties like cremini and shiitake.
- ▶ Finish with a sprinkle of fresh parsley or thyme.

Per Serving: 18 Calories; 0g Total Fat; 0g Saturated Fat; 0mg Cholesterol; 40mg Sodium; 3g Total Carbs; 1g Fiber; 2g Sugars; 2g Protein

Onion Rings

Servings: 4 | Prep Time: 10 Minutes | Cooking Time: 12 Minutes

Ingredients:

- 1 large (227g) onion
- 1/2 cup + 2 tbsp flour
- 1/2 teaspoon salt
- 1/2 cup + 2 tbsp beer
- 1 cup crushed panko breadcrumbs
- Oil for misting or cooking spray

Directions:

1. Peel onion, slice into rings and separate into rings.
2. In a bowl, mix flour and salt. Add beer and stir into a thick batter.
3. Coat onion rings in the batter.
4. Place breadcrumbs in a bag or container.
5. Remove rings from batter, shake off excess, then coat in breadcrumbs.
6. Arrange breaded rings on a tray. Mist with oil spray.
7. Place rings in air fryer basket in a single layer.
8. Cook at 199°C/390°F for 5 minutes. Shake, mist with oil, and cook 5 more minutes.
9. Shake, mist again and cook 2 more minutes until crispy.

Variations & Ingredients Tips:

- ▶ Use beer batter mix instead of making your own batter.
- ▶ Add cajun seasoning or ranch powder to the breading.
- ▶ Serve with ranch, barbecue sauce or chipotle mayo.

Per Serving: 240 Calories; 4g Total Fat; 1g Saturated Fat; 0mg Cholesterol; 374mg Sodium; 46g Total Carbs; 2g Fiber; 4g Sugars; 4g Protein

Rich Baked Sweet Potatoes

Servings: 2 | Prep Time: 5 Minutes | Cooking Time: 55 Minutes

Ingredients:

- 454g sweet potatoes, scrubbed and perforated with a fork
- 2 tsp olive oil
- Salt and pepper to taste
- 2 tbsp butter
- 3 tbsp honey

Directions:

1. Preheat air fryer at 204°C/400°F.
2. Mix olive oil, salt, pepper and honey in a bowl.
3. Brush the sweet potatoes all over with the honey oil mixture.
4. Place sweet potatoes in the air fryer basket and bake for 45 minutes, turning over halfway.
5. Let cool 10 minutes until cool enough to handle.
6. Slice each potato lengthwise and press ends together to open up slices.
7. Top with butter before serving.

Variations & Ingredients Tips:

- ▶ Add cinnamon, nutmeg or pumpkin spice to the honey oil mixture.
- ▶ Stuff baked sweet potatoes with sauteed spinach or black beans.
- ▶ Top with pecans, marshmallows or brown sugar before serving.

Per Serving: 291 Calories; 11g Total Fat; 4g Saturated Fat; 15mg Cholesterol; 115mg Sodium; 48g Total Carbs; 5g Fiber; 23g Sugars; 2g Protein

Five-spice Roasted Sweet Potatoes

Servings: 4 | Prep Time: 10 Minutes | Cooking Time: 12 Minutes

Ingredients:

- ½ teaspoon ground cinnamon
- ¼ teaspoon ground cumin
- ¼ teaspoon paprika
- 1 teaspoon chile powder
- ⅛ teaspoon turmeric
- ½ teaspoon salt (optional)
- Freshly ground black pepper
- 2 large sweet potatoes, peeled and cut into 2cm cubes (about 3 cups)

- 1 tablespoon olive oil

Directions:

1. In a large bowl, mix together cinnamon, cumin, paprika, chile powder, turmeric, salt, and pepper to taste.
2. Add potatoes and stir well.
3. Drizzle the seasoned potatoes with olive oil and stir until evenly coated.
4. Place seasoned potatoes in the air fryer baking pan or dish that fits basket.
5. Cook for 6 minutes at 198°C/390°F, stop and stir well.
6. Cook for an additional 6 minutes.

Variations & Ingredients Tips:

- Add a pinch of cayenne for extra heat.
- Toss with maple syrup before cooking.
- Sprinkle with sliced green onions after roasting.

Per Serving: Calories 150; Total Fat 4g; Saturated Fat 1g; Cholesterol 0mg; Sodium 200mg; Total Carbs 26g; Fiber 4g; Sugars 7g; Protein 2g

Sandwiches And Burgers Recipes

Thai-style Pork Sliders

Servings: 4 | Prep Time: 15 Minutes | Cooking Time: 15 Minutes

Ingredients:

- 310 grams Ground pork
- 2½ tablespoons Very thinly sliced scallions, white and green parts
- 4 teaspoons Minced peeled fresh ginger
- 2½ teaspoons Fish sauce (gluten-free, if a concern)
- 2 teaspoons Thai curry paste (see the headnote; gluten-free, if a concern)
- 2 teaspoons Light brown sugar
- ¾ teaspoon Ground black pepper
- 4 Slider buns (gluten-free, if a concern)

Directions:

1. Preheat the air fryer to 190°C/375°F.
2. Gently mix the pork, scallions, ginger, fish sauce, curry paste, brown sugar, and black pepper in a bowl until well combined. With clean, wet hands, form about 80 grams of the pork mixture into a slider about 6.5-cm in diameter. Repeat until you use up all the meat—3 sliders for the small batch, 4 for the medium, and 6 for the large. (Keep wetting your hands to help the patties adhere.)
3. When the machine is at temperature, set the sliders in the basket in one layer. Air-fry undisturbed for 14 minutes, or until the sliders are golden brown and caramelized at their edges and an instant-read meat thermometer inserted into the center of a slider registers 70°C/160°F.
4. Use a nonstick-safe spatula, and perhaps a flatware fork for balance, to transfer the sliders to a cutting board. Set the buns cut side down in the basket in one layer (working in batches as necessary) and air-fry undisturbed for 1 minute, to toast a bit and warm up. Serve the sliders warm in the buns.

Variations & Ingredients Tips:

- Use ground chicken or turkey for a leaner slider option.
- Substitute Thai curry paste with red curry paste or green curry paste for a different flavor profile.
- Serve with pickled vegetables, cilantro, and sriracha mayonnaise for extra Thai-inspired toppings.

Per Serving (1 slider): Calories: 240; Cholesterol: 65mg; Total Fat: 13g; Saturated Fat: 4g; Sodium: 490mg; Total Carbohydrates: 18g; Dietary Fiber: 1g; Total Sugars: 4g; Protein: 15g

Dijon Thyme Burgers

Servings: 3 | Prep Time: 15 Minutes | Cooking Time: 18 Minutes

Ingredients:

- 450 grams lean ground beef
- ⅓ cup panko breadcrumbs
- ¼ cup finely chopped onion
- 3 tablespoons Dijon mustard
- 1 tablespoon chopped fresh thyme
- 4 teaspoons Worcestershire sauce
- 1 teaspoon salt
- freshly ground black pepper
- Topping (optional):
- 2 tablespoons Dijon mustard
- 1 tablespoon dark brown sugar
- 1 teaspoon Worcestershire sauce
- 115 grams sliced Swiss cheese, optional

Directions:

1. Combine all the burger ingredients together in a large bowl and mix well. Divide the meat into 4 equal portions and then form the burgers, being careful not to over-handle the meat. One good way to do this is to throw the meat back and forth from one hand to another, packing the meat each time you catch it. Flatten the balls into patties, making an indentation in the center of each patty with your thumb (this will help it stay flat as it cooks) and flattening the sides of the burgers so that they will fit nicely into the air fryer basket.
2. Preheat the air fryer to 190°C/370°F.
3. If you don't have room for all four burgers, air-fry two or three burgers at a time for 8 minutes. Flip the burgers over and air-fry for another 6 minutes.
4. While the burgers are cooking combine the Dijon mustard, dark brown sugar, and Worcestershire sauce in a small bowl and mix well. This optional topping to the burgers really adds a boost of flavor at the end. Spread the Dijon topping evenly on each burger. If you cooked the burgers in batches, return the first batch to the cooker at this time – it's ok to place the fourth burger on top of the others in the center of the basket. Air-fry the burgers for another 3 minutes.
5. Finally, if desired, top each burger with a slice of Swiss cheese. Lower the air fryer temperature to 165°C/330°F and air-fry for another minute to melt the cheese. Serve the burgers on toasted brioche buns, dressed the way you like them.

Variations & Ingredients Tips:

- Use ground turkey or chicken for a leaner burger option.
- Add minced garlic or finely chopped herbs like parsley or chives for extra flavor.
- Substitute panko breadcrumbs with regular breadcrumbs or oats for a different texture.

Per Serving (1 burger with cheese): Calories: 500; Cholesterol: 120mg; Total Fat: 27g; Saturated Fat: 11g; Sodium: 1180mg; Total Carbohydrates: 21g; Dietary Fiber: 1g; Total Sugars: 5g; Protein: 41g

Reuben Sandwiches

Servings: 2 | Prep Time: 10 Minutes | Cooking Time: 11 Minutes

Ingredients:

- 225 grams Sliced deli corned beef
- 4 teaspoons Regular or low-fat mayonnaise (not fat-free)
- 4 Rye bread slices
- 2 tablespoons plus 2 teaspoons Russian dressing
- ½ cup Purchased sauerkraut, squeezed by the handful over the sink to get rid of excess moisture
- 55 grams (2 to 4 slices) Swiss cheese slices (optional)

Directions:

1. Set the corned beef in the basket, slip the basket into the machine, and heat the air fryer to 200°C/400°F. Air-fry undisturbed for 3 minutes from the time the basket is put in the machine, just to warm up the meat.
2. Use kitchen tongs to transfer the corned beef to a cutting board. Spread 1 teaspoon mayonnaise on one side of each slice of rye bread, rubbing the mayonnaise into the bread with a small flatware knife.
3. Place the bread slices mayonnaise side down on a cutting board. Spread the Russian dressing over the "dry" side of each slice. For one sandwich, top one slice of bread with the corned beef, sauerkraut, and cheese (if using). For two sandwiches, top two slices of bread each with half of the corned beef, sauerkraut, and cheese (if using). Close the sandwiches with the remaining bread, setting it mayonnaise side up on top.
4. Set the sandwich(es) in the basket and air-fry undisturbed for 8 minutes, or until browned and crunchy.
5. Use a nonstick-safe spatula, and perhaps a flatware fork for balance, to transfer the sandwich(es) to a cutting board. Cool for 2 or 3 minutes before slicing in half and serving.

Variations & Ingredients Tips:

- Substitute corned beef with pastrami for a classic New York deli taste.
- Use Thousand Island dressing instead of Russian dressing for a tangy, sweet flavor.
- Add sliced dill pickles or mustard to the sandwich for extra zing.

Per Serving (1 sandwich): Calories: 520; Cholesterol: 75mg; Total Fat: 30g; Saturated Fat: 9g; Sodium: 2020mg; Total Carbohydrates: 36g; Dietary Fiber: 4g; Total Sugars: 6g; Protein: 29g

Lamb Burgers

Servings: 3 | Prep Time: 15 Minutes | Cooking Time: 17 Minutes

Ingredients:

- 510 grams Ground lamb
- 3 tablespoons Crumbled feta
- 1 teaspoon Minced garlic
- 1 teaspoon Tomato paste

- ¾ teaspoon Ground coriander
- ¾ teaspoon Ground dried ginger
- Up to ⅛ teaspoon Cayenne
- Up to a ⅛ teaspoon Table salt (optional)
- 3 Kaiser rolls or hamburger buns (gluten-free, if a concern), split open

Directions:

1. Preheat the air fryer to 190°C/375°F.
2. Gently mix the ground lamb, feta, garlic, tomato paste, coriander, ginger, cayenne, and salt (if using) in a bowl until well combined, trying to keep the bits of cheese intact. Form this mixture into two 15-cm patties for the small batch, three 12.5-cm patties for the medium, or four 12.5-cm patties for the large.
3. Set the patties in the basket in one layer and air-fry undisturbed for 16 minutes, or until an instant-read meat thermometer inserted into one burger registers 70°C/160°F. (The cheese is not an issue with the temperature probe in this recipe as it was for the Inside-Out Cheeseburgers, because the feta is so well mixed into the ground meat.)
4. Use a nonstick-safe spatula, and perhaps a flatware fork for balance, to transfer the burgers to a cutting board. Set the buns cut side down in the basket in one layer (working in batches as necessary) and air-fry undisturbed for 1 minute, to toast a bit and warm up. Serve the burgers warm in the buns.

Variations & Ingredients Tips:

▶ Substitute feta with goat cheese or crumbled blue cheese for a different flavor profile.
▶ Add finely chopped mint or parsley to the lamb mixture for a fresh, herbal taste.
▶ Serve with tzatziki sauce, sliced cucumbers, and red onions for a Greek-inspired burger.

Per Serving (1 burger): Calories: 560; Cholesterol: 140mg; Total Fat: 34g; Saturated Fat: 15g; Sodium: 580mg; Total Carbohydrates: 25g; Dietary Fiber: 1g; Total Sugars: 3g; Protein: 38g

Asian Glazed Meatballs

Servings: 4 | Prep Time: 15 Minutes | Cooking Time: 10 Minutes

Ingredients:

- 1 large shallot, finely chopped
- 2 cloves garlic, minced
- 1 tablespoon grated fresh ginger
- 2 teaspoons fresh thyme, finely chopped
- 1½ cups brown mushrooms, very finely chopped (a food processor works well here)
- 2 tablespoons soy sauce
- freshly ground black pepper
- ½ kg ground beef
- ¼ kg ground pork
- 3 egg yolks
- 1 cup Thai sweet chili sauce (spring roll sauce)
- ¼ cup toasted sesame seeds
- 2 scallions, sliced

Directions:

1. Combine the shallot, garlic, ginger, thyme, mushrooms, soy sauce, freshly ground black pepper, ground beef and pork, and egg yolks in a bowl and mix the ingredients together. Gently shape the mixture into 24 balls, about the size of a golf ball.
2. Preheat the air fryer to 190°C/380°F.
3. Working in batches, air-fry the meatballs for 8 minutes, turning the meatballs over halfway through the cooking time. Drizzle some of the Thai sweet chili sauce on top of each meatball and return the basket to the air fryer, air-frying for another 2 minutes. Reserve the remaining Thai sweet chili sauce for serving.
4. As soon as the meatballs are done, sprinkle with toasted sesame seeds and transfer them to a serving platter. Scatter the scallions around and serve warm.
5. Variation and Ingredient Tips:
6. Use a food processor to finely chop the mushrooms for better texture in the meatballs.
7. Work in batches when air frying the meatballs to ensure even cooking and browning.
8. Drizzle the Thai sweet chili sauce over the meatballs towards the end of cooking for a nice glaze.
9. Per Serving: Calories: 550; Cholesterol: 205mg; Total Fat: 32g; Saturated Fat: 11g; Sodium: 1300mg; Total Carbohydrates: 36g; Dietary Fiber: 2g; Total Sugars: 23g; Protein: 29g
10. Chicken Apple Brie Melt
11. Servings: 3 | Prep Time: 10 Minutes | Cooking Time: 13 Minutes
12. Ingredients:
13. 3 140 to 170-gram boneless skinless chicken breasts
14. Vegetable oil spray
15. 1½ teaspoons Dried herbes de Provence
16. 85 grams Brie, rind removed, thinly sliced
17. 6 Thin cored apple slices
18. 3 French rolls (gluten-free, if a concern)
19. 2 tablespoons Dijon mustard (gluten-free, if a concern)
20. Directions:

1. Preheat the air fryer to 190°C/375°F.
2. Lightly coat all sides of the chicken breasts with vegeta-

ble oil spray. Sprinkle the breasts evenly with the herbes de Provence.

3. When the machine is at temperature, set the breasts in the basket and air-fry undisturbed for 10 minutes.
4. Top the chicken breasts with the apple slices, then the cheese. Air-fry undisturbed for 2 minutes, or until the cheese is melty and bubbling.
5. Use a nonstick-safe spatula and kitchen tongs, for balance, to transfer the breasts to a cutting board. Set the rolls in the basket and air-fry for 1 minute to warm through. (Putting them in the machine without splitting them keeps the insides very soft while the outside gets a little crunchy.)
6. Transfer the rolls to the cutting board. Split them open lengthwise, then spread 1 teaspoon mustard on each cut side. Set a prepared chicken breast on the bottom of a roll and close with its top, repeating as necessary to make additional sandwiches. Serve warm.

Variations & Ingredients Tips:

▶ Substitute the Brie with Camembert or another soft cheese of your choice.

▶ Use pears instead of apples for a different flavor profile.

▶ Add baby spinach or arugula for extra greens and nutrition.

Per Serving: Calories: 510; Cholesterol: 135mg; Total Fat: 19g; Saturated Fat: 8g; Sodium: 670mg; Total Carbohydrates: 41g; Dietary Fiber: 2g; Total Sugars: 6g; Protein: 45g

Chicken Saltimbocca Sandwiches

Servings: 3 | Prep Time: 10 Minutes | Cooking Time: 11 Minutes

Ingredients:

- 3 140to 170-gram boneless skinless chicken breasts
- 6 Thin prosciutto slices
- 6 Provolone cheese slices
- 3 Long soft rolls, such as hero, hoagie, or Italian sub rolls (gluten-free, if a concern), split open lengthwise
- 3 tablespoons Pesto, purchased or homemade (see the headnote)

Directions:

1. Preheat the air fryer to 200°C/400°F.
2. Wrap each chicken breast with 2 prosciutto slices, spiraling the prosciutto around the breast and overlapping the slices a bit to cover the breast. The prosciutto will stick to the chicken more readily than bacon does.
3. When the machine is at temperature, set the wrapped chicken breasts in the basket and air-fry undisturbed for 10 minutes, or until the prosciutto is frizzled and the chicken is cooked through.
4. Overlap 2 cheese slices on each breast. Air-fry undisturbed for 1 minute, or until melted. Take the basket out of the machine.
5. Smear the insides of the rolls with the pesto, then use kitchen tongs to put a wrapped and cheesy chicken breast in each roll.

Variations & Ingredients Tips:

▶ Use fresh mozzarella instead of provolone for a creamier texture.

▶ Add sliced tomatoes or roasted red peppers for extra flavor and nutrition.

▶ Substitute prosciutto with ham or bacon if desired.

Per Serving: Calories: 630; Cholesterol: 125mg; Total Fat: 32g; Saturated Fat: 11g; Sodium: 1580mg; Total Carbohydrates: 38g; Dietary Fiber: 2g; Total Sugars: 4g; Protein: 48g

Black Bean Veggie Burgers

Servings: 3 | Prep Time: 15 Minutes | Cooking Time: 10 Minutes

Ingredients:

- 1 cup Drained and rinsed canned black beans
- ⅓ cup Pecan pieces
- ⅓ cup Rolled oats (not quick-cooking or steel-cut; gluten-free, if a concern)
- 2 tablespoons (or 1 small egg) Pasteurized egg substitute, such as Egg Beaters (gluten-free, if a concern)
- 2 teaspoons Red ketchup-like chili sauce, such as Heinz
- ¼ teaspoon Ground cumin
- ¼ teaspoon Dried oregano
- ¼ teaspoon Table salt
- ¼ teaspoon Ground black pepper
- Olive oil
- Olive oil spray

Directions:

1. Preheat the air fryer to 200°C/400°F.
2. Put the beans, pecans, oats, egg substitute or egg, chili sauce, cumin, oregano, salt, and pepper in a food processor. Cover and process to a coarse paste that will hold its shape like sugar-cookie dough, adding olive oil in 1-teaspoon increments to get the mixture to blend smoothly. The amount of olive oil is actually dependent on the internal moisture content of the beans and the oats. Figure on about 1 tablespoon (three 1-teaspoon additions) for the smaller batch, with proportional increas-

es for the other batches. A little too much olive oil can't hurt, but a dry paste will fall apart as it cooks and a far-too-wet paste will stick to the basket.
3. Scrape down and remove the blade. Using clean, wet hands, form the paste into two 10 cm patties for the small batch, three 10 cm patties for the medium, or four 10 cm patties for the large batch, setting them one by one on a cutting board. Generously coat both sides of the patties with olive oil spray.
4. Set them in the basket in one layer. Air-fry undisturbed for 10 minutes, or until lightly browned and crisp at the edges.
5. Use a nonstick-safe spatula, and perhaps a flatware fork for balance, to transfer the burgers to a wire rack. Cool for 5 minutes before serving.

Variations & Ingredients Tips:

- Add finely chopped vegetables like bell peppers, onions, or carrots for extra flavor and nutrition.
- Experiment with different spices and herbs, such as smoked paprika, garlic powder, or cilantro.
- For a gluten-free version, ensure all ingredients are certified gluten-free.

Per Serving: Calories: 280; Cholesterol: 0mg; Total Fat: 15g; Saturated Fat: 2g; Sodium: 420mg; Total Carbohydrates: 28g; Dietary Fiber: 8g; Total Sugars: 2g; Protein: 10g

Perfect Burgers

Servings: 3 | Prep Time: 10 Minutes | Cooking Time: 13 Minutes

Ingredients:

- 510 grams 90% lean ground beef
- 1½ tablespoons Worcestershire sauce (gluten-free, if a concern)
- ½ teaspoon Ground black pepper
- 3 Hamburger buns (gluten-free if a concern), split open

Directions:

1. Preheat the air fryer to 190°C/375°F.
2. Gently mix the ground beef, Worcestershire sauce, and pepper in a bowl until well combined but preserving as much of the meat's fibers as possible. Divide this mixture into two 15-cm patties for the small batch, three 12.5-cm patties for the medium, or four 12.5-cm patties for the large. Make a thumbprint indentation in the center of each patty, about halfway through the meat.
3. Set the patties in the basket in one layer with some space between them. Air-fry undisturbed for 10 minutes, or until an instant-read meat thermometer inserted into the center of a burger registers 70°C/160°F (a medium-well burger). You may need to add 2 minutes cooking time if the air fryer is at 180°C/360°F.
4. Use a nonstick-safe spatula, and perhaps a flatware fork for balance, to transfer the burgers to a cutting board. Set the buns cut side down in the basket in one layer (working in batches as necessary) and air-fry undisturbed for 1 minute, to toast a bit and warm up. Serve the burgers in the warm buns.

Variations & Ingredients Tips:

- Mix in finely chopped onions, garlic, or herbs to the burger mixture for extra flavor.
- Use a mixture of ground beef and ground pork or lamb for a juicier, more flavorful burger.
- Top burgers with your favorite cheese, bacon, avocado, or sautéed mushrooms.

Per Serving (1 burger): Calories: 420; Cholesterol: 105mg; Total Fat: 22g; Saturated Fat: 8g; Sodium: 460mg; Total Carbohydrates: 23g; Dietary Fiber: 1g; Total Sugars: 3g; Protein: 34g

Salmon Burgers

Servings: 3 | Prep Time: 15 Minutes | Cooking Time: 8 Minutes

Ingredients:

- 510 grams Skinless salmon fillet, preferably fattier Atlantic salmon
- 1½ tablespoons Minced chives or the green part of a scallion
- ½ cup Plain panko bread crumbs (gluten-free, if a concern)
- 1½ teaspoons Dijon mustard (gluten-free, if a concern)
- 1½ teaspoons Drained and rinsed capers, minced
- 1½ teaspoons Lemon juice
- ¼ teaspoon Table salt
- ¼ teaspoon Ground black pepper
- Vegetable oil spray

Directions:

1. Preheat the air fryer to 190°C/375°F.
2. Cut the salmon into pieces that will fit in a food processor. Cover and pulse until coarsely chopped. Add the chives and pulse to combine, until the fish is ground but not a paste. Scrape down and remove the blade. Scrape the salmon mixture into a bowl. Add the bread crumbs, mustard, capers, lemon juice, salt, and pepper. Stir gently until well combined.
3. Use clean and dry hands to form the mixture into two 12.5-cm patties for a small batch, three 12.5-cm patties

for a medium batch, or four 12.5-cm patties for a large one.

4. Coat both sides of each patty with vegetable oil spray. Set them in the basket in one layer and air-fry undisturbed for 8 minutes, or until browned and an instant-read meat thermometer inserted into the center of a burger registers 65°C/145°F.
5. Use a nonstick-safe spatula, and perhaps a flatware fork for balance, to transfer the burgers to a wire rack. Cool for 2 or 3 minutes before serving.

Variations & Ingredients Tips:

- Substitute salmon with canned or leftover cooked salmon for convenience.
- Add finely chopped red bell pepper or celery to the burger mixture for extra crunch and flavor.
- Serve on toasted buns with lettuce, tomato, and a dollop of tartar sauce or remoulade.

Per Serving (1 burger): Calories: 320; Cholesterol: 95mg; Total Fat: 16g; Saturated Fat: 3g; Sodium: 440mg; Total Carbohydrates: 15g; Dietary Fiber: 1g; Total Sugars: 1g; Protein: 31g

Provolone Stuffed Meatballs

Servings: 4 | Prep Time: 20 Minutes | Cooking Time: 12 Minutes

Ingredients:

- 1 tablespoon olive oil
- 1 small onion, very finely chopped
- 1 to 2 cloves garlic, minced
- 340 grams ground beef
- 340 grams ground pork
- ¾ cup breadcrumbs
- ¼ cup grated Parmesan cheese
- ¼ cup finely chopped fresh parsley (or 1 tablespoon dried parsley)
- ½ teaspoon dried oregano
- 1½ teaspoons salt
- freshly ground black pepper
- 2 eggs, lightly beaten
- 140 grams sharp or aged provolone cheese, cut into 2.5-cm cubes

Directions:

1. Preheat a skillet over medium-high heat. Add the oil and cook the onion and garlic until tender, but not browned.
2. Transfer the onion and garlic to a large bowl and add the beef, pork, breadcrumbs, Parmesan cheese, parsley, oregano, salt, pepper and eggs. Mix well until all the ingredients are combined. Divide the mixture into 12 evenly sized balls. Make one meatball at a time, by pressing a hole in the meatball mixture with your finger and pushing a piece of provolone cheese into the hole. Mold the meat back into a ball, enclosing the cheese.
3. Preheat the air fryer to 190°C/380°F.
4. Working in two batches, transfer six of the meatballs to the air fryer basket and air-fry for 12 minutes, shaking the basket and turning the meatballs a couple of times during the cooking process. Repeat with the remaining six meatballs. You can pop the first batch of meatballs into the air fryer for the last two minutes of cooking to re-heat them. Serve warm.

Variations & Ingredients Tips:

- Substitute beef and pork with ground turkey or chicken for a leaner meatball option.
- Use mozzarella or fontina cheese instead of provolone for a milder flavor.
- Serve meatballs with marinara sauce, in sub rolls, or over pasta for a complete meal.

Per Serving (3 meatballs): Calories: 520; Cholesterol: 180mg; Total Fat: 36g; Saturated Fat: 15g; Sodium: 1160mg; Total Carbohydrates: 18g; Dietary Fiber: 1g; Total Sugars: 2g; Protein: 35g

Inside-out Cheeseburgers

Servings: 3 | Prep Time: 15 Minutes | Cooking Time: 9-11 Minutes

Ingredients:

- 510 grams 90% lean ground beef
- ¾ teaspoon Dried oregano
- ¾ teaspoon Table salt
- ¾ teaspoon Ground black pepper
- ¼ teaspoon Garlic powder
- 6 tablespoons (about 45 grams) Shredded Cheddar, Swiss, or other semi-firm cheese, or a purchased blend of shredded cheeses
- 3 Hamburger buns (gluten-free, if a concern), split open

Directions:

1. Preheat the air fryer to 190°C/375°F.
2. Gently mix the ground beef, oregano, salt, pepper, and garlic powder in a bowl until well combined without turning the mixture to mush. Form it into two 15-cm patties for the small batch, three for the medium, or four for the large.
3. Place 2 tablespoons of the shredded cheese in the center of each patty. With clean hands, fold the sides of the patty up to cover the cheese, then pick it up and roll it gently into a ball to seal the cheese inside. Gently press it back into a 12.5-cm burger without letting any cheese squish out. Continue filling and preparing more burgers,

as needed.

4. Place the burgers in the basket in one layer and air-fry undisturbed for 8 minutes for medium or 10 minutes for well-done. (An instant-read meat thermometer won't work for these burgers because it will hit the mostly melted cheese inside and offer a hotter temperature than the surrounding meat.)

5. Use a nonstick-safe spatula, and perhaps a flatware fork for balance, to transfer the burgers to a cutting board. Set the buns cut side down in the basket in one layer (working in batches as necessary) and air-fry undisturbed for 1 minute, to toast a bit and warm up. Cool the burgers a few minutes more, then serve them warm in the buns.

Variations & Ingredients Tips:

▶ Mix different types of cheese like cheddar, mozzarella, and blue cheese for a flavorful combination.

▶ Add finely chopped bacon or caramelized onions to the cheese stuffing for extra richness.

▶ Serve with your favorite burger toppings like lettuce, tomato, onion, and pickles.

Per Serving (1 burger): Calories: 480; Cholesterol: 125mg; Total Fat: 27g; Saturated Fat: 11g; Sodium: 720mg; Total Carbohydrates: 22g; Dietary Fiber: 1g; Total Sugars: 3g; Protein: 38g

Chicken Club Sandwiches

Servings: 3 | Prep Time: 15 Minutes | Cooking Time: 15 Minutes

Ingredients:

- 3 140- to 170-gram boneless skinless chicken breasts
- 6 Thick-cut bacon strips (gluten-free, if a concern)
- 3 Long soft rolls, such as hero, hoagie, or Italian sub rolls (gluten-free, if a concern)
- 3 tablespoons Regular, low-fat, or fat-free mayonnaise (gluten-free, if a concern)
- 3 Lettuce leaves, preferably romaine or iceberg
- 6 6-mm-thick tomato slices

Directions:

1. Preheat the air fryer to 190°C/375°F.

2. Wrap each chicken breast with 2 strips of bacon, spiraling the bacon around the meat, slightly overlapping the strips on each revolution. Start the second strip of bacon farther down the breast but on a line with the start of the first strip so they both end at a lined-up point on the chicken breast.

3. When the machine is at temperature, set the wrapped breasts bacon-seam side down in the basket with space between them. Air-fry undisturbed for 12 minutes, until the bacon is browned, crisp, and cooked through and an instant-read meat thermometer inserted into the center of a breast registers 75°C/165°F. You may need to add 2 minutes in the air fryer if the temperature is at 70°C/160°F.

4. Use kitchen tongs to transfer the breasts to a wire rack. Split the rolls open lengthwise and set them cut side down in the basket. Air-fry for 1 minute, or until warmed through.

5. Use kitchen tongs to transfer the rolls to a cutting board. Spread 1 tablespoon mayonnaise on the cut side of one half of each roll. Top with a chicken breast, lettuce leaf, and tomato slice. Serve warm.

Variations & Ingredients Tips:

▶ Use turkey bacon for a lower-fat option.

▶ Add sliced avocado or pickled onions for extra flavor and texture.

▶ Toast the rolls before assembling the sandwiches for a crispy texture.

Per Serving: Calories: 640; Cholesterol: 110mg; Total Fat: 34g; Saturated Fat: 9g; Sodium: 1180mg; Total Carbohydrates: 44g; Dietary Fiber: 2g; Total Sugars: 5g; Protein: 42g

Mexican Cheeseburgers

Servings: 4 | Prep Time: 20 Minutes | Cooking Time: 22 Minutes

Ingredients:

- 570 grams ground beef
- ¼ cup finely chopped onion
- ½ cup crushed yellow corn tortilla chips
- 1 (35-gram) packet taco seasoning
- ¼ cup canned diced green chilies
- 1 egg, lightly beaten
- 115 grams pepper jack cheese, grated
- 4 (30-cm) flour tortillas
- shredded lettuce, sour cream, guacamole, salsa (for topping)

Directions:

1. Combine the ground beef, minced onion, crushed tortilla chips, taco seasoning, green chilies, and egg in a large bowl. Mix thoroughly until combined – your hands are good tools for this. Divide the meat into four equal portions and shape each portion into an oval-shaped burger.

2. Preheat the air fryer to 190°C/370°F.

3. Air-fry the burgers for 18 minutes, turning them over halfway through the cooking time. Divide the cheese be-

tween the burgers, lower fryer to 170°C/340°F and air-fry for an additional 4 minutes to melt the cheese. (This will give you a burger that is medium-well. If you prefer your cheeseburger medium-rare, shorten the cooking time to about 15 minutes and then add the cheese and proceed with the recipe.)

4. While the burgers are cooking, warm the tortillas wrapped in aluminum foil in a 175°C/350°F oven, or in a skillet with a little oil over medium-high heat for a couple of minutes. Keep the tortillas warm until the burgers are ready.

5. To assemble the burgers, spread sour cream over three quarters of the tortillas and top each with some shredded lettuce and salsa. Place the Mexican cheeseburgers on the lettuce and top with guacamole. Fold the tortillas around the burger, starting with the bottom and then folding the sides in over the top. (A little sour cream can help hold the seam of the tortilla together.) Serve immediately.

Variations & Ingredients Tips:

▶ Use ground turkey or chicken for a leaner burger option.

▶ Substitute pepper jack cheese with Monterey Jack or cheddar cheese if preferred.

▶ Add sliced jalapeños or hot sauce to the burger mixture for extra heat.

Per Serving (1 burger): Calories: 780; Cholesterol: 165mg; Total Fat: 44g; Saturated Fat: 18g; Sodium: 1480mg; Total Carbohydrates: 51g; Dietary Fiber: 4g; Total Sugars: 4g; Protein: 46g

Eggplant Parmesan Subs

Servings: 2 | Prep Time: 10 Minutes | Cooking Time: 13 Minutes

Ingredients:

- 4 Peeled eggplant slices (about 1.25 cm thick and 7.5 cm in diameter)
- Olive oil spray
- 2 tablespoons plus 2 teaspoons Jarred pizza sauce, any variety except creamy
- ¼ cup (about 20 grams) Finely grated Parmesan cheese
- 2 Small, long soft rolls, such as hero, hoagie, or Italian sub rolls (gluten-free, if a concern), split open lengthwise

Directions:

1. Preheat the air fryer to 175°C/350°F.

2. When the machine is at temperature, coat both sides of the eggplant slices with olive oil spray. Set them in the basket in one layer and air-fry undisturbed for 10 minutes, until lightly browned and softened.

3. Increase the machine's temperature to 190°C/375°F (or 185°C/370°F, if that's the closest setting—unless the machine is already at 180°C/360°F, in which case leave it alone). Top each eggplant slice with 2 teaspoons pizza sauce, then 1 tablespoon of cheese. Air-fry undisturbed for 2 minutes, or until the cheese has melted.

4. Use a nonstick-safe spatula, and perhaps a flatware fork for balance, to transfer the eggplant slices cheese side up to a cutting board. Set the roll(s) cut side down in the basket in one layer (working in batches as necessary) and air-fry undisturbed for 1 minute, to toast the rolls a bit and warm them up. Set 2 eggplant slices in each warm roll.

Variations & Ingredients Tips:

▶ Use zucchini slices instead of eggplant for a different vegetable option.

▶ Add a slice of fresh mozzarella on top of the Parmesan for extra cheesiness.

▶ Sprinkle some dried herbs like oregano or basil on the eggplant before cooking for extra flavor.

Per Serving (1 sandwich): Calories: 280; Cholesterol: 10mg; Total Fat: 9g; Saturated Fat: 3g; Sodium: 840mg; Total Carbohydrates: 40g; Dietary Fiber: 5g; Total Sugars: 8g; Protein: 11g

Best-ever Roast Beef Sandwiches

Servings: 6 | Prep Time: 10 Minutes | Cooking Time: 30-50 Minutes

Ingredients:

- 2½ teaspoons Olive oil
- 1½ teaspoons Dried oregano
- 1½ teaspoons Dried thyme
- 1½ teaspoons Onion powder
- 1½ teaspoons Table salt
- 1½ teaspoons Ground black pepper
- 1 kg Beef eye of round
- 6 Round soft rolls, such as Kaiser rolls or hamburger buns (gluten-free if a concern), split open lengthwise
- ¾ cup Regular, low-fat or fat-free mayonnaise (gluten-free, if a concern)
- 6 Romaine lettuce leaves, rinsed
- 6 Round tomato slices (0.5 cm thick)

Directions:

1. Preheat the air fryer to 180°C/350°F.

2. Mix the oil, oregano, thyme, onion powder, salt, and pepper in a small bowl. Spread this mixture all over the eye of round.

3. When the machine is at temperature, set the beef in

the basket and air-fry for 30 to 50 minutes (the range depends on the size of the cut), turning the meat twice, until an instant-read meat thermometer inserted into the thickest piece of the meat registers 55°C/130°F for rare, 60°C/140°F for medium, or 65°C/150°F for well-done.

4. Use kitchen tongs to transfer the beef to a cutting board. Cool for 10 minutes. If serving now, carve into 3-mm-thick slices. Spread each roll with 2 tablespoons mayonnaise and divide the beef slices between the rolls. Top with a lettuce leaf and a tomato slice and serve. Or set the beef in a container, cover, and refrigerate for up to 3 days to make cold roast beef sandwiches anytime.

Variations & Ingredients Tips:

- Experiment with different herbs and spices in the rub, such as garlic powder, paprika, or rosemary.
- Add sliced red onions or pickles for extra flavor and crunch.
- Use leftover roast beef for cold sandwiches or salads.

Per Serving: Calories: 560; Cholesterol: 115mg; Total Fat: 27g; Saturated Fat: 6g; Sodium: 980mg; Total Carbohydrates: 32g; Dietary Fiber: 2g; Total Sugars: 4g; Protein: 47g

Chili Cheese Dogs

Servings: 3 | Prep Time: 10 Minutes | Cooking Time: 12 Minutes

Ingredients:

- 340 grams Lean ground beef
- 1½ tablespoons Chile powder
- 240 grams plus 2 tablespoons Jarred sofrito
- 3 Hot dogs (gluten-free, if a concern)
- 3 Hot dog buns (gluten-free, if a concern), split open lengthwise
- 3 tablespoons Finely chopped scallion
- 60 grams Shredded Cheddar cheese

Directions:

1. Crumble the ground beef into a medium or large saucepan set over medium heat. Brown well, stirring often to break up the clumps. Add the chile powder and cook for 30 seconds, stirring the whole time. Stir in the sofrito and bring to a simmer. Reduce the heat to low and simmer, stirring occasionally, for 5 minutes. Keep warm.
2. Preheat the air fryer to 200°C/400°F.
3. When the machine is at temperature, put the hot dogs in the basket and air-fry undisturbed for 10 minutes, or until the hot dogs are bubbling and blistered, even a little crisp.
4. Use kitchen tongs to put the hot dogs in the buns. Top each with about 120 grams of the ground beef mixture, 1 tablespoon of the minced scallion, and 20 grams of the cheese. (The scallion should go under the cheese so it superheats and wilts a bit.) Set the filled hot dog buns in the basket and air-fry undisturbed for 2 minutes, or until the cheese has melted.
5. Remove the basket from the machine. Cool the chili cheese dogs in the basket for 5 minutes before serving.

Variations & Ingredients Tips:

- Use turkey or veggie hot dogs for a healthier option.
- Substitute cheddar cheese with your favorite melty cheese, such as pepper jack or Swiss.
- Add diced onions or jalapeños to the chili for extra flavor and heat.

Per Serving: Calories: 580; Cholesterol: 110mg; Total Fat: 32g; Saturated Fat: 13g; Sodium: 1420mg; Total Carbohydrates: 36g; Dietary Fiber: 5g; Total Sugars: 6g; Protein: 38g

White Bean Veggie Burgers

Servings: 3 | Prep Time: 15 Minutes | Cooking Time: 13 Minutes

Ingredients:

- 320 grams Drained and rinsed canned white beans
- 3 tablespoons Rolled oats (not quick-cooking or steel-cut; gluten-free, if a concern)
- 3 tablespoons Chopped walnuts
- 2 teaspoons Olive oil
- 2 teaspoons Lemon juice
- 1½ teaspoons Dijon mustard (gluten-free, if a concern)
- ¾ teaspoon Dried sage leaves
- ¼ teaspoon Table salt
- Olive oil spray
- 3 Whole-wheat buns or gluten-free whole-grain buns (if a concern), split open

Directions:

1. Preheat the air fryer to 200°C/400°F.
2. Place the beans, oats, walnuts, oil, lemon juice, mustard, sage, and salt in a food processor. Cover and process to make a coarse paste that will hold its shape, about like wet sugar-cookie dough, stopping the machine to scrape down the inside of the canister at least once.
3. Scrape down and remove the blade. With clean and wet hands, form the bean paste into two 10-cm patties for the small batch, three 10-cm patties for the medium, or four 10-cm patties for the large batch. Generously coat the patties on both sides with olive oil spray.
4. Set them in the basket with some space between them

and air-fry undisturbed for 12 minutes, or until lightly brown and crisp at the edges. The tops of the burgers will feel firm to the touch.

5. Use a nonstick-safe spatula, and perhaps a flatware fork for balance, to transfer the burgers to a cutting board. Set the buns cut side down in the basket in one layer (working in batches as necessary) and air-fry undisturbed for 1 minute, to toast a bit and warm up. Serve the burgers warm in the buns.

Variations & Ingredients Tips:

- Use black beans, chickpeas, or lentils instead of white beans for a different flavor and color.
- Add grated carrots, zucchini, or beets to the burger mixture for extra nutrition and texture.
- Serve with your favorite burger toppings like lettuce, tomato, onion, and pickles.

Per Serving (1 burger): Calories: 350; Cholesterol: 0mg; Total Fat: 13g; Saturated Fat: 1g; Sodium: 520mg; Total Carbohydrates: 48g; Dietary Fiber: 9g; Total Sugars: 4g; Protein: 14g

Crunchy Falafel Balls

Servings: 8 | Prep Time: 15 Minutes | Cooking Time: 16 Minutes

Ingredients:

- 600 grams Drained and rinsed canned chickpeas
- 60 grams Olive oil
- 3 tablespoons All-purpose flour
- 1½ teaspoons Dried oregano
- 1½ teaspoons Dried sage leaves
- 1½ teaspoons Dried thyme
- ¾ teaspoon Table salt
- Olive oil spray

Directions:

1. Preheat the air fryer to 200°C/400°F.
2. Place the chickpeas, olive oil, flour, oregano, sage, thyme, and salt in a food processor. Cover and process into a paste, stopping the machine at least once to scrape down the inside of the canister.
3. Scrape down and remove the blade. Using clean, wet hands, form 2 tablespoons of the paste into a ball, then continue making 9 more balls for a small batch, 15 more for a medium one, and 19 more for a large batch. Generously coat the balls in olive oil spray.
4. Set the balls in the basket in one layer with a little space between them and air-fry undisturbed for 16 minutes, or until well browned and crisp.
5. Dump the contents of the basket onto a wire rack. Cool for 5 minutes before serving.

Variations & Ingredients Tips:

- Add minced garlic, onion, or herbs like parsley or cilantro for extra flavor.
- Serve with tahini sauce, hummus, or tzatziki for dipping.
- Make a falafel sandwich by stuffing pita bread with falafel balls, lettuce, tomato, and sauce.

Per Serving (2 falafel balls): Calories: 170; Cholesterol: 0mg; Total Fat: 9g; Saturated Fat: 1g; Sodium: 230mg; Total Carbohydrates: 18g; Dietary Fiber: 4g; Total Sugars: 2g; Protein: 5g

Sausage And Pepper Heros

Servings: 3 | Prep Time: 10 Minutes | Cooking Time: 11 Minutes

Ingredients:

- 3 links (about 255 grams total) Sweet Italian sausages (gluten-free, if a concern)
- 1½ Medium red or green bell pepper(s), stemmed, cored, and cut into 1.25-cm-wide strips
- 1 medium Yellow or white onion(s), peeled, halved, and sliced into thin half-moons
- 3 Long soft rolls, such as hero, hoagie, or Italian sub rolls (gluten-free, if a concern), split open lengthwise
- For garnishing Balsamic vinegar
- For garnishing Fresh basil leaves

Directions:

1. Preheat the air fryer to 200°C/400°F.
2. When the machine is at temperature, set the sausage links in the basket in one layer and air-fry undisturbed for 5 minutes.
3. Add the pepper strips and onions. Continue air-frying, tossing and rearranging everything about once every minute, for 5 minutes, or until the sausages are browned and an instant-read meat thermometer inserted into one of the links registers 70°C/160°F.
4. Use a nonstick-safe spatula and kitchen tongs to transfer the sausages and vegetables to a cutting board. Set the rolls cut side down in the basket in one layer (working in batches as necessary) and air-fry undisturbed for 1 minute, to toast the rolls a bit and warm them up. Set 1 sausage with some pepper strips and onions in each warm roll, sprinkle balsamic vinegar over the sandwich fillings, and garnish with basil leaves.

Variations & Ingredients Tips:

- Use hot Italian sausage or chorizo for a spicier sandwich.
- Add sliced mushrooms or zucchini to the pepper and onion mixture for extra veggies.
- Top with shredded mozzarella or provolone cheese for a cheesy twist.

Per Serving (1 sandwich): Calories: 560; Cholesterol: 60mg; Total Fat: 36g; Saturated Fat: 12g; Sodium: 1420mg; Total Carbohydrates: 39g; Dietary Fiber: 3g; Total Sugars: 7g; Protein: 24g

Desserts And Sweets

Holiday Peppermint Cake

Servings: 4 | Prep Time: 10 Minutes | Cooking Time: 20 Minutes

Ingredients:
- 1 1/2 cups flour
- 3 eggs
- 1/3 cup molasses
- 1/2 cup olive oil
- 1/2 cup almond milk
- 1/2 tsp vanilla extract
- 1/2 tsp peppermint extract
- 1 tsp baking powder
- 1/2 tsp salt

Directions:
1. Preheat air fryer to 190°C/380°F.
2. Whisk the eggs and molasses until smooth.
3. Slowly mix in olive oil, almond milk, vanilla and peppermint extracts.
4. In another bowl, sift together flour, baking powder and salt.
5. Gradually incorporate dry ingredients into wet ingredients until combined.
6. Pour batter into a greased baking pan and place in air fryer basket.
7. Bake for 12-15 minutes until a toothpick inserted comes out clean.
8. Serve and enjoy!

Variations & Ingredients Tips:
- Use coconut or vegetable oil instead of olive oil.
- Add crushed peppermint candies or chocolate chips to the batter.
- Top with peppermint frosting or whipped cream.

Per Serving: Calories: 538; Total Fat: 27g; Saturated Fat: 4g; Sodium: 307mg; Total Carbohydrates: 67g; Dietary Fiber: 2g; Total Sugars: 28g; Protein: 8g

Mango Cobbler With Raspberries

Servings: 4 | Prep Time: 15 Minutes | Cooking Time: 30 Minutes

Ingredients:
- 1 1/2 cups chopped mango
- 1 cup raspberries
- 1 tbsp brown sugar
- 2 tsp cornstarch
- 1 tsp lemon juice
- 2 tbsp sunflower oil
- 1 tbsp maple syrup
- 1 tsp vanilla
- 1/2 cup rolled oats
- 1/3 cup flour
- 3 tbsp coconut sugar
- 1 tsp cinnamon
- 1/4 tsp nutmeg
- 1/8 tsp salt

Directions:
1. In a baking pan, mix mango, raspberries, brown sugar, cornstarch and lemon juice.
2. In another bowl, mix oil, maple syrup, vanilla, oats, flour, coconut sugar, cinnamon, nutmeg and salt.
3. Sprinkle oat mixture evenly over fruit filling.
4. Preheat air fryer to 160°C/320°F.
5. Bake for 20 minutes until topping is golden.
6. Enjoy warm.

Variations & Ingredients Tips:
- Use other fruit combinations like peach-blueberry or apple-cranberry.
- Top with vanilla ice cream or whipped cream.
- Add chopped nuts like pecans or walnuts to the topping.

Per Serving: Calories: 271; Total Fat: 8g; Saturated Fat: 1g; Sodium: 53mg; Total Carbohydrates: 49g; Dietary Fiber: 6g; Total Sugars: 26g; Protein: 4g

Dark Chocolate Cream Galette

Servings: 4 | Prep Time: 15 Minutes | Cooking Time: 55 Minutes + Cooling Time

Ingredients:

- 454 grams cream cheese, softened
- 1 cup crumbled graham crackers
- 1 cup dark cocoa powder
- ½ cup white sugar
- 1 tsp peppermint extract
- 1 tsp ground cinnamon
- 1 egg
- 1 cup condensed milk
- 2 tbsp muscovado sugar
- 1 ½ tsp butter, melted

Directions:

1. Preheat air fryer to 180°C/350°F.
2. Place the crumbled graham crackers in a large bowl and stir in the muscovado sugar and melted butter. Spread the mixture into a greased pie pan, pressing down to form the galette base.
3. Place the pan into the air fryer and Bake for 5 minutes. Remove the pan and set aside.
4. Place the cocoa powder, cream cheese, peppermint extract, white sugar, cinnamon, condensed milk, and egg in a large bowl and whip thoroughly to combine.
5. Spoon the chocolate mixture over the graham cracker crust and level the top with a spatula. Put in the air fryer and Bake for 40 minutes until firm.
6. Transfer the galette to a wire rack to cool. Serve and enjoy!

Variations & Ingredients Tips:

- ▶ Use milk chocolate or white chocolate instead of dark for a sweeter flavor.
- ▶ Add espresso powder or instant coffee to the filling for a mocha twist.
- ▶ Top with fresh berries, whipped cream, or a dusting of powdered sugar.

Per Serving: Calories: 780; Total Fat: 50g; Saturated Fat: 29g; Sodium: 510mg; Total Carbohydrates: 77g; Dietary Fiber: 5g; Total Sugars: 61g; Protein: 15g

Apple Dumplings

Servings: 4 | Prep Time: 20 Minutes | Cooking Time: 25 Minutes

Ingredients:

- 1 Basic Pie Dough (see the following recipe)
- 4 medium Granny Smith or Pink Lady apples, peeled and cored
- 4 tablespoons sugar
- 4 teaspoons cinnamon
- 1/2 teaspoon ground nutmeg
- 4 tablespoons unsalted butter, melted
- 4 scoops ice cream, for serving

Directions:

1. Preheat the air fryer to 165°C/330°F.
2. Bring the pie crust recipe to room temperature.
3. Place the pie crust on a floured surface. Divide the dough into 4 equal pieces. Roll out each piece to 0.6cm-thick rounds.
4. Place an apple onto each dough round. Sprinkle 1 tablespoon of sugar in the core part of each apple; sprinkle 1 teaspoon cinnamon and 1/8 teaspoon nutmeg over each. Place 1 tablespoon of butter into the center of each.
5. Fold up the sides and fully cover the cored apples.
6. Place the dumplings into the air fryer basket and spray with cooking spray. Cook for 25 minutes. Check after 14 minutes cooking; if they're getting too brown, reduce the heat to 160°C/320°F and complete the cooking.
7. Serve hot apple dumplings with a scoop of ice cream.

Variations & Ingredients Tips:

- ▶ Use different apple varieties like Honeycrisp or Fuji.
- ▶ Add raisins or chopped nuts to the filling.
- ▶ Drizzle with caramel sauce before serving.

Per Serving: Calories: 375; Total Fat: 18g; Saturated Fat: 10g; Sodium: 195mg; Total Carbohydrates: 51g; Dietary Fiber: 4g; Total Sugars: 29g; Protein: 3g

Donut Holes

Servings: 13 | Prep Time: 15 Minutes | Cooking Time: 12 Minutes

Ingredients:

- 6 tablespoons Granulated white sugar
- 1½ tablespoons Butter, melted and cooled
- 2 tablespoons (or 1 small egg, well beaten) Pasteurized egg substitute, such as Egg Beaters
- 6 tablespoons Regular or low-fat sour cream (not fat-free)
- ¾ teaspoon Vanilla extract
- 1⅔ cups All-purpose flour
- ¾ teaspoon Baking powder
- ¼ teaspoon Table salt
- Vegetable oil spray

Directions:

1. Preheat the air fryer to 180°C/350°F.
2. Whisk the sugar and melted butter in a medium bowl until well combined. Whisk in the egg substitute or egg, then the sour cream and vanilla until smooth. Remove the whisk and stir in the flour, baking powder, and salt with a wooden spoon just until a soft dough forms.
3. Use 2 tablespoons of this dough to create a ball between your clean palms. Set it aside and continue making

balls: 8 more for the small batch, 12 more for the medium batch, or 17 more for the large one.

4. Coat the balls in the vegetable oil spray, then set them in the basket with as much air space between them as possible. Even a fraction of 0.25 cm will be enough, but they should not touch. Air-fry undisturbed for 12 minutes, or until browned and cooked through. A toothpick inserted into the center of a ball should come out clean.

5. Pour the contents of the basket onto a wire rack. Cool for at least 5 minutes before serving.

Variations & Ingredients Tips:

▶ Toss the warm donut holes in cinnamon sugar or powdered sugar.

▶ Add grated lemon or orange zest to the batter for a citrusy flavor.

▶ Fill the donut holes with jam, Nutella, or pastry cream using a piping bag.

Per Serving: Calories: 130; Total Fat: 5g; Saturated Fat: 3g; Sodium: 100mg; Total Carbohydrates: 20g; Dietary Fiber: 0g; Total Sugars: 9g; Protein: 2g

Coconut-custard Pie

Servings: 4 | Prep Time: 10 Minutes | Cooking Time: 20 Minutes

Ingredients:

- 1 cup milk
- ¼ cup plus 2 tablespoons sugar
- ¼ cup biscuit baking mix
- 1 teaspoon vanilla
- 2 eggs
- 2 tablespoons melted butter
- cooking spray
- ½ cup shredded, sweetened coconut

Directions:

1. Place all ingredients except coconut in a medium bowl.
2. Using a hand mixer, beat on high speed for 3 minutes.
3. Let sit for 5 minutes.
4. Preheat air fryer to 165°C/330°F.
5. Spray a 15-cm round or 15x15-cm square baking pan with cooking spray and place pan in air fryer basket.
6. Pour filling into pan and sprinkle coconut over top.
7. Cook pie at 165°C/330°F for 20 minutes or until center sets.

Variations & Ingredients Tips:

▶ Use coconut milk instead of regular milk for a more intense coconut flavor.

▶ Add a pinch of nutmeg or cinnamon to the filling.

▶ Serve with a scoop of vanilla ice cream or a dollop of whipped cream.

Per Serving: Calories: 310; Total Fat: 15g; Saturated Fat: 10g; Sodium: 260mg; Total Carbohydrates: 39g; Dietary Fiber: 1g; Total Sugars: 30g; Protein: 6g

Giant Buttery Chocolate Chip Cookie

Servings: 4 | Prep Time: 15 Minutes | Cooking Time: 16 Minutes

Ingredients:

- ⅔ cup plus 1 tablespoon All-purpose flour
- ¼ teaspoon Baking soda
- ¼ teaspoon Table salt
- Baking spray
- 4 tablespoons (¼ cup/½ stick) plus 1 teaspoon Butter, at room temperature
- ¼ cup plus 1 teaspoon Packed dark brown sugar
- 3 tablespoons plus 1 teaspoon Granulated white sugar
- 2½ tablespoons Pasteurized egg substitute, such as Egg Beaters
- ½ teaspoon Vanilla extract
- ¾ cup plus 1 tablespoon Semisweet or bittersweet chocolate chips

Directions:

1. Preheat the air fryer to 180°C/350°F.
2. Whisk the flour, baking soda, and salt in a bowl until well combined.
3. For a small air fryer, coat the inside of a 15-cm round cake pan with baking spray. For a medium air fryer, coat the inside of an 18-cm round cake pan with baking spray. And for a large air fryer, coat the inside of a 20-cm round cake pan with baking spray.
4. Using a hand electric mixer at medium speed, beat the butter, brown sugar, and granulated white sugar in a bowl until smooth and thick, about 3 minutes, scraping down the inside of the bowl several times.
5. Beat in the pasteurized egg substitute or egg (as applicable) and vanilla until uniform. Scrape down and remove the beaters. Fold in the flour mixture and chocolate chips with a rubber spatula, just until combined. Scrape and gently press this dough into the prepared pan, getting it even across the pan to the perimeter.
6. Set the pan in the basket and air-fry undisturbed for 16 minutes, or until the cookie is puffed, browned, and feels set to the touch.
7. Transfer the pan to a wire rack and cool for 10 minutes. Loosen the cookie from the perimeter with a spatula,

then invert the pan onto a cutting board and let the cookie come free. Remove the pan and reinvert the cookie onto the wire rack. Cool for 5 minutes more before slicing into wedges to serve.

Variations & Ingredients Tips:

- ▶ Use white chocolate chips, peanut butter chips, or M&Ms instead of regular chocolate chips.
- ▶ Add chopped nuts like walnuts, pecans, or macadamia nuts to the dough.
- ▶ Sprinkle with flaky sea salt before baking for a sweet-salty flavor.

Per Serving: Calories: 490; Total Fat: 26g; Saturated Fat: 15g; Sodium: 270mg; Total Carbohydrates: 62g; Dietary Fiber: 3g; Total Sugars: 39g; Protein: 5g

Spanish Churro Bites

Servings: 5 | Prep Time: 15 Minutes | Cooking Time: 35 Minutes

Ingredients:

- 1/4 tsp salt
- 2 tbsp vegetable oil
- 3 tbsp white sugar
- 1 cup flour
- 1/2 tsp ground cinnamon
- 2 tbsp granulated sugar

Directions:

1. On the stovetop, add 1 cup of water, salt, 1 tbsp of vegetable oil and 1 tbsp sugar in a pot. Bring to a boil over high heat.
2. Remove from the heat and add flour. Stir with a wooden spoon until the flour is combined and a ball of dough forms. Cool for 5 minutes.
3. Put the ball of dough in a plastic pastry bag with a star tip. Squeeze the dough to the tip and twist the top of the bag. Squeeze 10 strips of dough, about 13cm long each, onto a workspace. Spray with cooking oil.
4. Preheat air fryer to 170°C/340°F.
5. Place the churros in the greased frying basket and Air Fry for 22-25 minutes, flipping once halfway through until golden.
6. Meanwhile, heat the remaining vegetable oil in a small bowl. In another shallow bowl, mix the remaining 2 tbsp sugar and cinnamon.
7. Roll the cooked churros in cinnamon sugar. Top with granulated sugar and serve immediately.

Variations & Ingredients Tips:

- ▶ Serve with a thick hot chocolate or caramel dipping sauce.
- ▶ Add a teaspoon of vanilla extract to the dough.
- ▶ Stuff with chocolate or cream filling after baking.

Per serving: Calories: 235; Total Fat: 6g; Saturated Fat: 1g; Cholesterol: 0mg; Sodium: 135mg; Total Carbs: 42g; Dietary Fiber: 1g; Total Sugars: 10g; Protein: 4g

Struffoli

Servings: 10 | Prep Time: 45 Minutes | Cooking Time: 20 Minutes

Ingredients:

- 1/4 cup butter, softened
- 2/3 cup sugar
- 5 eggs
- 2 teaspoons vanilla extract
- Zest of 1 lemon
- 4 cups all-purpose flour
- 2 teaspoons baking soda
- 1/4 teaspoon salt
- 480-g honey
- 1 teaspoon ground cinnamon
- Zest of 1 orange
- 2 tablespoons water
- Nonpareils candy sprinkles

Directions:

1. Cream the butter and sugar together in a bowl until light and fluffy using a hand mixer. Add the eggs, vanilla and lemon zest and mix.
2. In a separate bowl, combine the flour, baking soda and salt. Add the dry ingredients to the wet ingredients and mix until you have a soft dough.
3. Shape the dough into a ball, wrap it in plastic and let it rest for 30 minutes.
4. Divide the dough ball into four pieces. Roll each piece into a long rope. Cut each rope into about 25 (1.3cm) pieces. Roll each piece into a tight ball. You should have 100 little balls when finished.
5. Preheat the air fryer to 190°C/370°F.
6. In batches of about 20, transfer the dough balls to the air fryer basket, leaving a small space in between them. Air-fry the dough balls at 190°C/370°F for 3 to 4 minutes, shaking the basket when one minute of cooking time remains.
7. After all the dough balls are air-fried, make the honey topping. Melt the honey in a small saucepan on the stovetop. Add the cinnamon, orange zest, and water Simmer for one minute.
8. Place the air-fried dough balls in a large bowl and drizzle the honey mixture over top. Gently toss to coat all the dough balls evenly.
9. Transfer the coated struffoli to a platter and sprinkle the

nonpareil candy sprinkles over top. You can dress the presentation up by piling the balls into the shape of a wreath or pile them high in a cone shape to resemble a Christmas tree.

10. Struffoli can be made ahead. Store covered tightly.

Variations & Ingredients Tips:

- Substitute lemon or orange extract for the vanilla.
- Add a shot of liqueur like anisette or rum to the honey coating.
- Rolled in powdered sugar instead of coated in honey.

Per serving: Calories: 385; Total Fat: 8g; Saturated Fat: 4g; Cholesterol: 105mg; Sodium: 310mg; Total Carbs: 72g; Dietary Fiber: 2g; Total Sugars: 34g; Protein: 7g

Sea-salted Caramel Cookie Cups

Servings: 12 | Prep Time: 10 Minutes | Cooking Time: 12 Minutes

Ingredients:

- 1/3 cup butter
- 1/4 cup brown sugar
- 1 teaspoon vanilla extract
- 1 large egg
- 1 cup all-purpose flour
- 1/2 cup old-fashioned oats
- 1/2 teaspoon baking soda
- 1/4 teaspoon salt
- 1/3 cup sea-salted caramel chips

Directions:

1. Preheat the air fryer to 150°C/300°F.
2. In a large bowl, cream the butter with the brown sugar and vanilla. Whisk in the egg and set aside.
3. In a separate bowl, mix the flour, oats, baking soda, and salt. Then gently mix the dry ingredients into the wet. Fold in the caramel chips.
4. Divide the batter into 12 silicon muffin liners. Place the cookie cups into the air fryer basket and cook for 12 minutes or until a toothpick inserted in the center comes out clean.
5. Remove and let cool 5 minutes before serving.

Variations & Ingredients Tips:

- Use chocolate chips or white chocolate chips instead of caramel chips.
- Add chopped nuts like pecans or walnuts to the batter.
- Drizzle with extra caramel sauce after baking.

Per serving: Calories: 160; Total Fat: 7g; Saturated Fat: 4g; Cholesterol: 30mg; Sodium: 150mg; Total Carbs: 22g; Dietary Fiber: 1g; Total Sugars: 10g; Protein: 2g

Glazed Cherry Turnovers

Servings: 8 | Prep Time: 20 Minutes | Cooking Time: 14 Minutes

Ingredients:

- 2 sheets frozen puff pastry, thawed
- 1 (595-gram) can premium cherry pie filling
- 2 teaspoons ground cinnamon
- 1 egg, beaten
- 1 cup sliced almonds
- 1 cup powdered sugar
- 2 tablespoons milk

Directions:

1. Roll a sheet of puff pastry out into a square that is approximately 25-cm by 25-cm. Cut this large square into quarters.
2. Mix the cherry pie filling and cinnamon together in a bowl. Spoon ¼ cup of the cherry filling into the center of each puff pastry square. Brush the perimeter of the pastry square with the egg wash. Fold one corner of the puff pastry over the cherry pie filling towards the opposite corner, forming a triangle. Seal the two edges of the pastry together with the tip of a fork, making a design with the tines. Brush the top of the turnovers with the egg wash and sprinkle sliced almonds over each one. Repeat these steps with the second sheet of puff pastry. You should have eight turnovers at the end.
3. Preheat the air fryer to 190°C/370°F.
4. Air-fry two turnovers at a time for 14 minutes, carefully turning them over halfway through the cooking time.
5. While the turnovers are cooking, make the glaze by whisking the powdered sugar and milk together in a small bowl until smooth. Let the glaze sit for a minute so the sugar can absorb the milk. If the consistency is still too thick to drizzle, add a little more milk, a drop at a time, and stir until smooth.
6. Let the cooked cherry turnovers sit for at least 10 minutes. Then drizzle the glaze over each turnover in a zigzag motion. Serve warm or at room temperature.

Variations & Ingredients Tips:

- Use different pie fillings like apple, blueberry, or peach.
- Substitute sliced almonds with chopped pecans or walnuts.
- Serve with a scoop of vanilla ice cream or a dollop of whipped cream.

Per Serving: Calories: 460; Total Fat: 24g; Saturated Fat: 5g; Sodium: 200mg; Total Carbohydrates: 57g; Dietary Fiber: 3g; Total Sugars: 30g; Protein: 8g

Nutty Cookies

Servings: 6 | Prep Time: 10 Minutes | Cooking Time: 25 Minutes

Ingredients:

- 1/4 cup pistachios
- 1/4 cup evaporated cane sugar
- 1/4 cup raw almonds
- 1/2 cup almond flour
- 1 tsp pure vanilla extract
- 1 egg white

Directions:

1. Preheat air fryer to 190°C/375°F.
2. Add 1/4 cup of pistachios and almonds into a food processor. Pulse until they resemble crumbles.
3. Roughly chop the rest of the pistachios with a sharp knife.
4. Combine all ingredients in a large bowl until completely incorporated.
5. Form 6 equally-sized balls and transfer to the parchment-lined frying basket. Allow for 2.5-cm between each portion.
6. Bake for 7 minutes. Cool on a wire rack for 5 minutes. Serve and enjoy.

Variations & Ingredients Tips:

- Substitute other nuts like walnuts or pecans for some of the nuts.
- Add 1/4 cup dried fruit like cranberries or cherries.
- Drizzle with melted chocolate after cooling.

Per serving: Calories: 190; Total Fat: 13g; Saturated Fat: 1g; Cholesterol: 0mg; Sodium: 25mg; Total Carbs: 14g; Dietary Fiber: 3g; Total Sugars: 8g; Protein: 6g

Orange-chocolate Cake

Servings: 6 | Prep Time: 15 Minutes | Cooking Time: 35 Minutes

Ingredients:

- 3/4 cup flour
- 1/2 cup sugar
- 7 tbsp cocoa powder
- 1/2 tsp baking soda
- 1/2 cup milk
- 2 1/2 tbsp sunflower oil
- 1/2 tbsp orange juice
- 2 tsp vanilla
- 2 tsp orange zest
- 3 tbsp butter, softened
- 1 1/4 cups powdered sugar

Directions:

1. Use a whisk to combine the flour, sugar, 2 tbsp of cocoa powder, baking soda, and a pinch of salt in a bowl. Once combined, add milk, sunflower oil, orange juice, and orange zest. Stir until combined.
2. Preheat the air fryer to 175°C/350°F. Pour the batter into a greased cake pan and Bake for 25 minutes or until a knife inserted in the center comes out clean.
3. Use an electric beater to beat the butter and powdered sugar together in a bowl. Add the remaining cocoa powder and vanilla and whip until fluffy. Scrape the sides occasionally. Refrigerate until ready to use.
4. Allow the cake to cool completely, then run a knife around the edges of the baking pan. Turn it upside-down on a plate so it can be frosted on the sides and top. When the frosting is no longer cold, use a butter knife or small spatula to frost the sides and top. Cut into slices and enjoy!

Variations & Ingredients Tips:

- Substitute orange juice and zest with lemon for a lemon-chocolate cake.
- Top with chocolate shavings or orange slices for garnish.
- Make cupcakes by dividing batter into a muffin pan.

Per serving: Calories: 320; Total Fat: 16g; Saturated Fat: 6g; Cholesterol: 20mg; Sodium: 150mg; Total Carbs: 44g; Dietary Fiber: 2g; Total Sugars: 30g; Protein: 4g

Mom's Amaretto Cheesecake

Servings: 6 | Prep Time: 20 Minutes | Cooking Time: 35 Minutes

Ingredients:

- 2/3 cup slivered almonds
- 1/2 cup Corn Chex
- 1 tbsp light brown sugar
- 3 tbsp butter, melted
- 400g cream cheese
- 2 tbsp sour cream
- 1/2 cup granulated sugar
- 1/2 cup Amaretto liqueur
- 1/2 tsp lemon juice
- 2 tbsp almond flakes

Directions:

1. In a food processor, pulse corn Chex, almonds, and brown sugar until it has a powdered consistency. Transfer it to a bowl. Stir in melted butter with a fork until butter is well distributed. Press mixture into a greased 20cm cake pan.

2. Preheat air fryer to 200°C/400°F.
3. In a bowl, combine cream cheese, sour cream, granulated sugar, Amaretto liqueur, and lemon juice until smooth. Pour it over the crust and cover with aluminum foil.
4. Place springform pan in the air fryer basket and bake for 16 minutes. Remove the foil and cook for 6 more minutes until a little jiggly in the center.
5. Let sit covered in the fridge for at least 2 hours. Release side of pan and serve sprinkled with almond flakes.

Variations & Ingredients Tips:

▶ Use vanilla wafers or graham crackers instead of Corn Chex for the crust.

▶ Substitute Amaretto with 5ml almond extract for a non-alcoholic version.

▶ Top with fresh berries or a drizzle of chocolate sauce before serving.

Per serving: Calories: 520; Total Fat: 38g; Saturated Fat: 20g; Cholesterol: 100mg; Sodium: 310mg; Total Carbs: 32g; Dietary Fiber: 2g; Total Sugars: 25g; Protein: 9g

Fried Twinkies

Servings: 6 | Prep Time: 20 Minutes | Cooking Time: 5 Minutes

Ingredients:
- 2 Large egg white(s)
- 2 tablespoons Water
- 1½ cups (about 255 grams) Ground gingersnap cookie crumbs
- 6 Twinkies
- Vegetable oil spray

Directions:

1. Preheat the air fryer to 200°C/400°F.
2. Set up and fill two shallow soup plates or small pie plates on your counter: one for the egg white(s), whisked with the water until foamy; and one for the gingersnap crumbs.
3. Dip a Twinkie in the egg white(s), turning it to coat on all sides, even the ends. Let the excess egg white mixture slip back into the rest, then set the Twinkie in the crumbs. Roll it to coat on all sides, even the ends, pressing gently to get an even coating. Then repeat this process: egg white(s), followed by crumbs. Lightly coat the prepared Twinkie on all sides with vegetable oil spray. Set aside and coat each of the remaining Twinkies with the same double-dipping technique, followed by spraying.
4. Set the Twinkies flat side up in the basket with as much air space between them as possible. Air-fry for 5 minutes, or until browned and crunchy.
5. Use a nonstick-safe spatula to gently transfer the Twinkies to a wire rack. Cool for at least 10 minutes before serving.

Variations & Ingredients Tips:

▶ Substitute gingersnaps with graham crackers, shortbread cookies, or vanilla wafers.

▶ Fill the Twinkies with jam, peanut butter, or chocolate ganache before coating.

▶ Dust with powdered sugar or drizzle with honey before serving.

Per Serving: Calories: 340; Total Fat: 15g; Saturated Fat: 4.5g; Sodium: 270mg; Total Carbohydrates: 48g; Dietary Fiber: 1g; Total Sugars: 30g; Protein: 3g

Sultana & Walnut Stuffed Apples

Servings: 4 | Prep Time: 10 Minutes | Cooking Time: 30 Minutes

Ingredients:
- 4 apples, cored and halved
- 2 tablespoons lemon juice
- 1/4 cup sultana raisins
- 3 tablespoons chopped walnuts
- 3 tablespoons dried cranberries
- 2 tablespoons packed brown sugar
- 1/3 cup apple cider
- 1 tablespoon cinnamon

Directions:

1. Preheat air fryer to 175°C/350°F.
2. Spritz the apples with lemon juice and put them in a baking pan.
3. Combine the raisins, cinnamon, walnuts, cranberries, and brown sugar, then spoon 1/4 of the mix into the apples.
4. Drizzle the apple cider around the apples, Bake for 13-18 minutes until softened.
5. Serve warm.

Variations & Ingredients Tips:

▶ Use other dried fruits like apricots, dates or prunes.

▶ Add a pinch of nutmeg or allspice to the spice mix.

▶ Drizzle with honey or maple syrup before serving.

Per serving: Calories: 230; Total Fat: 6g; Saturated Fat: 1g; Cholesterol: 0mg; Sodium: 15mg;

Total Carbs: 45g; Dietary Fiber: 5g; Total Sugars: 35g; Protein: 3g

Mango-chocolate Custard

Servings: 4 | Prep Time: 15 Minutes | Cooking Time: 40 Minutes

Ingredients:

- 4 egg yolks
- 2 tbsp granulated sugar
- 1/8 tsp almond extract
- 1 1/2 cups half-and-half
- 3/4 cup chocolate chips
- 1 mango, pureed
- 1 mango, chopped
- 1 tsp fresh mint, chopped

Directions:

1. Beat egg yolks, sugar and almond extract. Set aside.
2. Warm half-and-half in a saucepan until simmering.
3. Whisk some half-and-half into egg mixture, then whisk egg mixture into saucepan.
4. Stir in chocolate chips and mango puree for 10 mins until melted.
5. Divide custard into 4 ramekins.
6. Preheat air fryer to 175°C/350°F.
7. Bake ramekins for 6-8 minutes.
8. Cool, then chill in fridge for 2 hours up to 2 days.
9. Serve topped with chopped mango and mint.

Variations & Ingredients Tips:

- ▶ Use coconut milk instead of half-and-half.
- ▶ Add a splash of rum or orange liqueur.
- ▶ Top with toasted coconut or crushed cookies.

Per Serving: Calories: 350; Total Fat: 21g; Saturated Fat: 11g; Sodium: 62mg; Total Carbohydrates: 35g; Dietary Fiber: 3g; Total Sugars: 27g; Protein: 7g

Fast Brownies

Servings: 4 | Prep Time: 10 Minutes | Cooking Time: 25 Minutes

Ingredients:

- ½ cup flour
- 2 tbsp cocoa
- 1/3 cup granulated sugar
- ¼ tsp baking soda
- 3 tbsp butter, melted
- 1 egg
- ¼ tsp salt
- ½ cup chocolate chips
- ¼ cup chopped hazelnuts
- 1 tbsp powdered sugar
- 1 tsp vanilla extract

Directions:

1. Preheat air fryer at 180°C/350°F.
2. Combine all ingredients, except chocolate chips, hazelnuts, and powdered sugar, in a bowl.
3. Fold in chocolate chips and pecans.
4. Press mixture into a greased cake pan.
5. Place cake pan in the air fryer basket and Bake for 12 minutes.
6. Let cool for 10 minutes before slicing into 9 brownies.
7. Scatter with powdered sugar and serve.

Variations & Ingredients Tips:

- ▶ Use white chocolate chips and macadamia nuts for a blondie version.
- ▶ Add a swirl of peanut butter or Nutella to the batter before baking.
- ▶ Serve with a drizzle of salted caramel sauce or a dollop of vanilla ice cream.

Per Serving: Calories: 400; Total Fat: 22g; Saturated Fat: 10g; Sodium: 280mg; Total Carbohydrates: 50g; Dietary Fiber: 3g; Total Sugars: 34g; Protein: 5g

Honeyed Tortilla Fritters

Servings: 8 | Prep Time: 10 Minutes | Cooking Time: 10 Minutes

Ingredients:

- 2 tbsp granulated sugar
- 1/2 tsp ground cinnamon
- 1 tsp vanilla powder
- Salt to taste
- 8 flour tortillas, quartered
- 2 tbsp butter, melted
- 4 tsp honey
- 1 tbsp almond flakes

Directions:

1. Preheat air fryer at 200°C/400°F.
2. Mix sugar, cinnamon, vanilla powder and salt in a bowl.
3. Brush tortilla quarters with melted butter and coat in sugar mixture.
4. Place tortillas in air fryer basket and cook for 4 mins, flipping once.
5. Transfer to a plate and let cool 5 mins until hardened.
6. Drizzle with honey and sprinkle with almond flakes before serving.

Variations & Ingredients Tips:

- ▶ Use corn tortillas instead of flour for a crunchier texture.
- ▶ Add ground ginger or nutmeg to the spice mix.
- ▶ Serve with caramel or chocolate dipping sauce.

Per Serving (4 fritters): Calories: 188; Total Fat: 8g; Saturated Fat: 3g; Sodium: 200mg; Total Carbohydrates: 27g; Dietary Fiber: 2g; Total Sugars: 11g; Protein: 3g

Vanilla-strawberry Muffins

Servings: 4 | Prep Time: 10 Minutes | Cooking Time: 25 Minutes

Ingredients:

- 1/4 cup diced strawberries
- 2 tbsp powdered sugar
- 1 cup flour
- 1/2 tsp baking soda
- 1/3 cup granulated sugar
- 1/4 tsp salt
- 1 tsp vanilla extract
- 1 egg
- 1 tbsp butter, melted
- 1/2 cup diced strawberries
- 2 tbsp chopped walnuts
- 6 tbsp butter, softened
- 1 1/2 cups powdered sugar
- 1/8 tsp peppermint extract

Directions:

1. Preheat air fryer at 190°C/375°F.
2. Combine flour, baking soda, granulated sugar, and salt in a bowl.
3. In another bowl, combine the vanilla, egg, walnuts and melted butter.
4. Pour wet ingredients into dry ingredients and toss to combine.
5. Fold in half of the strawberries and spoon mixture into 8 greased silicone cupcake liners.
6. Place cupcakes in the frying basket and Bake for 6-8 minutes.
7. Let cool onto a cooling rack for 10 minutes.
8. Blend the remaining strawberries in a food processor until smooth.
9. Slowly add powdered sugar to softened butter while beating in a bowl. Stir in peppermint extract and puréed strawberries until blended.
10. Spread over cooled cupcakes. Serve sprinkled with powdered sugar.

Variations & Ingredients Tips:

▶ Use other berries like raspberries or blueberries instead of strawberries.

▶ Add lemon or orange zest to the batter.

▶ Top with cream cheese frosting instead of strawberry buttercream.

Per serving (2 muffins): Calories: 510; Total Fat: 18g; Saturated Fat: 9g; Cholesterol: 70mg; Sodium: 280mg; Total Carbs: 83g; Dietary Fiber: 2g; Total Sugars: 57g; Protein: 5g

INDEX

A

Acorn Squash Halves With Maple Butter Glaze 65

Air-fried Turkey Breast With Cherry Glaze 34

Apple Cornbread Stuffed Pork Loin With Apple Gravy 44

Apple Dumplings 80

Aromatic Pork Tenderloin 41

Asian Glazed Meatballs 71

Asian Sweet Chili Chicken 32

Avocado Fries 26

B

Bagels With Avocado & Tomatoes 17

Balsamic Beet Chips 63

Basil Cheese & Ham Stromboli 38

Basil Crab Cakes With Fresh Salad 48

Basil Green Beans 56

Beef Fajitas 41

Best-ever Brussels Sprouts 65

Best-ever Roast Beef Sandwiches 76

Black Bean Veggie Burgers 72

Boneless Ribeyes 43

Breakfast Chimichangas 18

British Fish & Chips 52

Broccoli & Mushroom Beef 38

Buffalo Bites 27

Buttered Swordfish Steaks 47

C

Californian Tilapia 53

Carrot Chips 27

Cheddar Bean Taquitos 56

Cheddar-ham-corn Muffins 16

Cheesy Eggplant Rounds 58

Cheesy Veggie Frittata 55

Chicken Club Sandwiches 75

Chicken Cordon Bleu Patties 33

Chicken Meatballs With A Surprise 32

Chicken Parmesan 33

Chicken Saltimbocca Sandwiches 72

Chicken Souvlaki Gyros 29

Chili Cheese Dogs 77

Chocolate Chip Banana Muffins 18

Coconut-custard Pie 81

Coffee-rubbed Pork Tenderloin 43

Colorful French Toast Sticks 13

Country-style Pork Ribs(2) 40

Crispy Chicken Cakes 20

Crispy Curried Sweet Potato Fries 23

Crispy Duck With Cherry Sauce 34

Crispy Herbed Potatoes 62

Crispy Smoked Pork Chops 41

Crunchy Falafel Balls 78

Crunchy Rice Paper Samosas 54

Curried Chicken Legs 37

D

Dark Chocolate Cream Galette 79

Dijon Thyme Burgers 69

Dilly Sesame Roasted Asparagus 66

Donut Holes 80

E

Easy Caprese Flatbread 16

Easy Scallops With Lemon Butter 46

Easy Tex-mex Chimichangas 45

Easy Zucchini Lasagna Roll-ups 54

Eggplant Parmesan 55

Eggplant Parmesan Subs 76

Extra Crispy Country-style Pork Riblets 45

F

Fake Shepherd´s Pie 54

Fast Brownies 86

Fennel & Chicken Ratatouille 32

Feta & Shrimp Pita 47

Fish Cakes 51

Fish Tortillas With Coleslaw 50

Fish-in-chips 49

Five-spice Roasted Sweet Potatoes 68

French Grouper Nicoise 47

French Toast And Turkey Sausage Roll-ups 15

French-style Pork Medallions 42

Fried Olives 24

Fried Peaches 24

Fried Twinkies 85

G

Garam Masala Cauliflower Pakoras 23

Garlic-butter Lobster Tails 52

Giant Buttery Chocolate Chip Cookie 81

Gingery Turkey Meatballs 35

Glazed Cherry Turnovers 83

Golden Breaded Mushrooms 58

Green Egg Quiche 20

H

Hashbrown Potatoes Lyonnaise 19

Hearty Salad 56

Herbed Zucchini Poppers 66

Holiday Lobster Salad 50

Holiday Peppermint Cake 79

Home-style Cinnamon Rolls 56

Honey Mustard Pork Roast 39

Honey-mustard Roasted Cabbage 67

Honeyed Tortilla Fritters 86

Hot Garlic Kale Chips 21

Huevos Rancheros 18

I

Inside-out Cheeseburgers 74

J

Jalapeño & Mozzarella Stuffed Mushrooms 21

Japanese-style Turkey Meatballs 31

Jerk Chicken Drumsticks 30

K

Kale Chips 22

Katsu Chicken Thighs 36

Kid's Flounder Fingers 48

L

Lamb Burgers 70

Lime Muffins 15

M

Mahi Mahi With Cilantro-chili Butter 49

Mango Cobbler With Raspberries 79

Mango-chocolate Custard 86

Maple Balsamic Glazed Salmon 52

Matcha Granola 14

Mediterranean Egg Sandwich 17

Mediterranean Roasted Vegetables 63

Mexican Cheeseburgers 75

Mini Everything Bagels 13

Mom's Amaretto Cheesecake 84

Mom's Potatoes Au Gratin 65

Mushrooms, Sautéed 67

N

Nutty Cookies 84

Nutty Whole Wheat Muffins 13

O

Old Bay Fish `n´ Chips 51

Onion Rings 68

Orange Glazed Pork Tenderloin 43

Orange Rolls.. 17

Orange-chocolate Cake 84

Original Köttbullar 39

P

Pecan Turkey Cutlets.. 36

Perfect Burgers... 73

Philly Chicken Cheesesteak Stromboli 29

Poppy Seed Mini Hot Dog Rolls 22

Pork & Beef Egg Rolls.. 42

Pork Tenderloin Salad 64

Potato-wrapped Salmon Fillets 50

Provolone Stuffed Meatballs 74

Pumpkin Bread With Walnuts 15

R

Ranch Chips 28

Reuben Sandwiches 70

Rich Baked Sweet Potatoes 68

Roasted Corn Salad.. 62

Roasted Red Pepper Dip 23

Roasted Tomatillo Salsa 25

Rosemary Garlic Goat Cheese 26

S

Salmon Burgers 73

Saucy Shrimp 46

Sausage And Pepper Heros 78

Sea-salted Caramel Cookie Cups 83

Sesame Orange Tofu With Snow Peas 60

Sesame-crusted Tuna Steaks 46

Shrimp Pirogues 25

Shrimp Po'boy With Remoulade Sauce 48

Sloppy Joes 39

Soft Pretzels 14

Southern Okra Chips 62

Southern-fried Chicken Livers 31

Spanish Churro Bites 82

Spiced Vegetable Galette 57

Steak Fries 63

Steakhouse Baked Potatoes 67

Steakhouse Burgers With Red Onion Compote 37

Struffoli 82

Stuffed Zucchini Boats 60

Sultana & Walnut Stuffed Apples 85

Sushi-style Deviled Eggs 57

Sweet Corn Bread 59

Sweet-and-salty Pretzels 21

T

Tandoori Cauliflower 66

Tandoori Lamb Samosas 40

Tex-mex Potatoes With Avocado Dressing 58

Thai-style Pork Sliders 69

The Rise of Air Fryers: A Brief History and Evolution in British Kitchens 10

The Science Behind Air Fryer Cooking: A Culinary Revolution 11

The Versatility of Air Fryers: From Crispy Snacks to Gourmet Meals 12

Thick-crust Pepperoni Pizza 27

Tortilla Crusted Chicken Breast 34

Turkey Bacon Dates 22

Turkey-hummus Wraps 31

Two-cheese Grilled Sandwiches 61

V

Vanilla-strawberry Muffins 87

Vegetarian Stuffed Bell Peppers 59

Veggie-stuffed Bell Peppers 60

W

Wasabi-coated Pork Loin Chops 38

White Bean Veggie Burgers 77

Wilted Brussels Sprout Slaw 64

Windsor's Chicken Salad 35

Y

Yogurt-marinated Chicken Legs 29

Z

Zucchini Fries With Roasted Garlic Aïoli 26

Zucchini Hash Browns 19

Printed in Great Britain
by Amazon